The Opinion Function

The Opinion Function:

Editorial and Interpretive Writing for the News Media

John L. Hulteng
University of Oregon

Harper & Row, Publishers
New York, Evanston, San Francisco, London

To B. J.

Contents

The Opinion Function

1
The Ubiquitous Ingredient

Heard through the clamor of conversation and the drifting blue smoke of a cocktail party: "... and that's all there is to it—we've got to take a firm stand and tell them to 'like it or lump it.' "

Over the neighbor's back hedge, on a summer afternoon: "... if you ask me, she's up to something, and poor Fred will be the last one to find out."

From the syndicated columnist in the evening paper: "White House sources are apparently convinced that the next presidential election will be decided by events abroad rather than conditions in this country."

And in the pear-shaped tones of the TV news commentator: "... so for the moment, the rioting is ended. But for how long? What spark will set off the next round, perhaps next week, perhaps tomorrow?"

At all levels of communication, from the one-to-one relationship of the conversational exchange to the few-to-many flow involved in the workings of the mass media, the ingredient of opinion is invariably present. Sometimes it constitutes only a shading, an overlay on the core of information that is being transmitted. Sometimes it is the principal element involved. Sometimes it stands out openly and bluntly. Sometimes it is unwittingly or deliberately concealed, masked as fact. Sometimes it is conveyed indirectly, by the way in which a news story is positioned on a page or by the ironic lift of the TV announcer's eyebrow as he quotes a statement from the mayor.

Of the many purposes that communication serves, that of conveying opinion so as to shape the reactions and thinking of others is one of the most significant.

Advertisers, propagandists, preachers, and teachers all are case makers in varying degree, attempting to mold the attitudes and actions of a few or a multitude. Friends offering counsel, politicians seeking votes, the entertainer doing a satirical monologue—all are engaged in fusing opinion with information in the hope that as a result a viewpoint will be changed or a course of action altered.

Much opinion interchange takes place in casual conversation, in small group meetings, in the classroom, at the legislature, and in an infinitude of other situations in which persons interact. This book is not concerned with such forms of opinion trading. It deals with the exercise of the opinion function in the mass media—newspapers, radio, television, and magazines.

The opinion ingredient is introduced into these media in a variety of ways. Advertising is a major and specialized form of case making and opinion changing, a field by itself; it will not be taken up in this book, except in passing.

THE VISIBLE PERSUADERS

There are also various hidden persuaders who function through the mass media, but not as openly as advertisers. They seek to make their impact on readers or viewers by "planting" points of view in what may seem on the surface to be news accounts; or they seek to manipulate the elements of a news situation so that only selected ones come to the public's attention, conveying a biased or half true impression of the reality. The activities and the tactics of such propagandists are also outside the purview of this book.

What the book *does* deal with is the spectrum of visible persuasion in the mass media. Much of the nonadvertising, nonentertainment content of the newspapers, magazines, and to a lesser extent the broadcast media, represents various kinds of efforts to explain, analyze, or interpret the news. These efforts are aimed at bringing about better reader or viewer understanding, winning acceptance of a particular interpretation or viewpoint, or promoting some kind of action on the part of those who are reached by the persuasive message.

Such efforts take a variety of forms. Some are framed as editorials, the "this is what *we* think" view of the newspaper, magazine, or broadcast station, clearly labeled as such. Some are in the form of background or interpretive news analyses, interspersed with straight news reports. Some are reflective essays, as in *Time.* Some are lengthy, graph-studded summaries of a complex situation, as in *U.S. News & World Report,* or in comparable broadcast form as a CBS or NBC documentary. Some are full-length magazine articles. Some are pictorial—editorial cartoons or photographs. Some are in the form of the signed opinions of a single syndicated columnist. Some are a blend of book review and persuasive case making, as in *Saturday Review* or the *New York Times Book Review*. And some are the product of exponents of the journalism of advocacy, who mix reporting and urgent opinion in proportions that are difficult for the consumer to identify or sort out.

These are the visible persuaders—some a good deal more visible than others. And it is the way that they carry out the opinion function of the mass media that this book will explore.

SERVING A NEED

As has been noted, the efforts of the visible persuaders—in various forms—make up a significant part of the content of the mass media. These efforts serve a need of the consumers of the mass media products. Most of us these days are drowning in data. There is an overwhelming glut of information on every hand, on every topic.

As Nick Williams, editor of the *Los Angeles Times,* observed, "Most of us find our brains numbed by masses of contradictory, unrelated information. On many of the major problems of our time, most of us are mental dropouts—confused, unable to start sorting out the facts and unable to organize them toward any solutions."[1]

The findings of researchers in the field of opinion formation and attitude change indicate that only rarely does anyone come to a conclusion solely because of exposure to more and more information on the subject under consideration.[2] Most of us need additional help along a different dimension if we are to start sorting out the facts and organizing them toward solutions.

We need exposure to the opinions of others—and not just the opinions of those with an ax to grind, the political leaders, the special-interest spokesmen. We need the aid we can get from the analysis and interpretation provided by persons who are steeped in the flow of events but who can keep those events in reasonably dispassionate perspective. The writers, commentators, cartoonists, and columnists of the mass media fill that role for a vast number of Americans. In some instances, they fill it ably. In others, of course, they perform less successfully and serve only to add to the confusion and accelerate the dropout trend that Williams identified.

The purpose of this book is to help nurture new generations of writers and analysts who will continue the opinion function of the mass media. Perhaps they will be able to make it more useful—more consistently useful—to the readers, listeners, and viewers who are in a very real sense dependent on that opinion function as they try to find their way through the bewildering confusion of events and ideas that surrounds them daily.

NOTES

1. In an article by Nick Williams, "The Balking Begins Only When We Start to Define What the Public Interest Is," in the *Bulletin of the American Society of Newspaper Editors,* March 1971, p. 17.

2. "There is a substantial body of research findings indicating that cognition—knowing something new—increasing information—is effective as an attitude change agent only under very specialized conditions. One such condition is that the issue being discussed be a new one, with no prior relationship to the individual's already-formed attitudes. It is a rare kind of issue which meets this requirement." Marvin Karlins and Herbert I. Abelson, *Persuasion,* New York, Springer Publishing Co., 1970, p. 33.

2
Some Background

There have been eras in which the opinion function has been the chief preoccupation—almost the only preoccupation—of the journalistic media. The pamphleteers and writers of broadsides in colonial days dealt more in argument and persuasion than in information. The editors of the era of the partisan press, during the first half of the nineteenth century, deployed all the resources of their publications, news columns as well as editorials, in advocacy of the political party or cause they had chosen. The reader then didn't even try to sort fact from opinion; the two were blended on every page, in every paragraph. This was true to a considerable extent also during the period of yellow journalism at the close of the nineteenth century.

The editorial page or editorial column, as a specially designated place for the expression of the editor's opinion, came into being more than 100 years ago. But it was not until the acceptance by the press of the concept of objective news reporting, during the first quarter of the twentieth century, that a general and consistent effort was made to separate news from opinion in the newspaper. The pattern of separation later carried over into the broadcast media and to some extent into magazines.

There still exist publications that concern themselves largely or exclusively with opinion, of course. Magazines such as the *Nation*, the *New Republic*, and *National Review* are in this category, together with much of the underground or counterculture press. Characteristically, such publications speak to the already converted, those of like view.

Most of the present-day media, however, serve a variety of needs, and the provision of analysis and opinion is only one of their functions.

They also purvey information, advertising, and entertainment, in vary-ing mixes. And most of today's editors and broadcasters make an effort to signal to the reader, listener, or viewer when they put on the pundit's hat and start handing down judgments and prophecies. They make that effort, however, only on the basis of an individual, internal decision that they best serve the consumer that way; there is no journalistic equivalent of the Pure Food and Drugs Act to ensure honest labeling.

THE SUBJECTIVITY SCALE

Some observers of the press have suggested that media content can be plotted along a continuum or spectrum according to the relative degree of objectivity and subjectivity it contains. At one end of the continuum they would put *straight news reporting*—the transmission of the basic determinable facts about a news situation.

Next on the scale, moving away from the objective ideal, would be the *feature article*—whether in print or on the broadcast media—which seeks to highlight the human interest values in a news event.

Then would come *interpretive* or *background reporting,* which probes behind the surface facts and brings supplementary information to bear to make more understandable a complex development or situation.

A notch further would be *reviewing* or *criticism,* in which the writer passes judgment on the quality of some kind of art offering: book, play, movie, or recital.

And next would be *editorial writing*—making an argument to be used in print or on the air with the purpose of changing an attitude or explaining what something means, in the judgment of the writer.

And, finally, at the subjective end of the scale, would be the *syndi-cated columnist* who deals almost entirely in case making and the ex-pression of opinion, often without the backstopping of argumentation and evidence that characterizes editorial writing. (Presumably he shares that spot on the scale with the opinion magazine editor and the under-ground press newsman, whose theme is chiefly attack.)

Such a scale is appealing because it is neat and orderly. It may also be misleading if taken too literally. As a practical matter, the categories blur and blend into each other, and the opinion function can show up to some degree everywhere on the continuum.

Perhaps the most realistic view is to acknowledge that the media today do make an effort to segregate and compartmentalize news and opinion. But the compartments aren't airtight by any means.

NO AUTOMATIC HEARING

The scale also helps to suggest the changing relationship of the journalist to his audience as he moves along the spectrum from straight news reporting to editorializing.

So long as he is engaged in reporting the news as objectively as he can manage (and of course there is no such animal as total objectivity this side of the Pearly Gates) the newsman is, in effect, armored in righteousness. He is Helping to Inform the Public, Making the Representative System of Democracy Work, Keeping a Watchful Eye on the Public Business.

But as the newsman turns to editorial writing, venturing along the subjectivity scale more and more into opinion territory, he leaves behind some of his protections and justifications. He begins sticking his neck out, quite a long way out. He is not simply identifying and reporting facts any longer; now he is saying to his reader or viewer: "This is what this latest development means" or "Now, this is what you ought to think—or do—about this or that situation, or issue, or person, or sacred cow."

The citizen at the receiving end, who might with gratitude and docility accept the services of the news reporter, views in quite a different light the editorial writer or the columnist. To these he is more than likely to respond: "Just who does that character think he is, telling me what to think, or do, or believe?"

Anyone who would exercise the opinion function for any of the mass media ought to be prepared to establish his credentials with his audience if he hopes to get a hearing. He can't expect that hearing just because he wears the label "editorial writer," even though his colleague in the reporting ranks may indeed enjoy an automatic acceptance as bearer of objective tidings.

ONCE THERE WERE GIANTS . . .

This built-in skepticism and resistance on the part of the audience so far as the opinion content of the mass media is concerned somewhat limit the leverage of these media in changing the attitudes of the public. That the press still does have a significant leverage is pretty generally acknowledged, but it is usually diffuse and difficult to measure.

And certainly that leverage is exerted in a fashion different from that of a century or a half century ago. In those days, the predecessors of today's editors, columnists, and broadcasters wielded a great deal of clout as individual opinion leaders. The circumstances then were, of course, altogether different from those of today. The leading editors of the period had the media field to themselves; they were national figures.

Horace Greeley spoke with so powerful a voice through his *New York Tribune* that he was able to orchestrate at least a part of the battle strategy of the Civil War.[1] Near the turn of the century, Joseph Pulitzer, with his *New York World,* and William Randolph Hearst, with his *New York Journal,* managed to generate a war fever on a national basis and pave the way for American entry into hostilities with Spain.[2]

Today few editors possess such personal influence, and in fact few are widely known outside their own communities or even their own offices unless they somehow have acquired celebrity in some other dimension. (William Buckley, editor of the magazine *National Review,* has achieved national attention as a political candidate and as spokesman for a conservative viewpoint.) The editors' competitors in the broadcast media are more often likely to be celebrities. But commentators such as Walter Cronkite are influential chiefly as reporters—interpretive reporters, to be sure—rather than as editorial thunderers in the old tradition. (Edward R. Murrow was something of an exception.)

The influence of the present day media is exerted in a variety of ways, not just in the accents of the editor or owners. Some results of the opinion molding of newspapers, magazines, or broadcast networks can be measured, although imperfectly and approximately; others can only be guessed at. (We'll look a bit later at some research in this area.)

One wry acknowledgment of the leverage of the opinion framers came from one in their ranks, the syndicated columnist Nicholas von Hoffman:

> We, too, have heard about the power of the press, the thunder of the fourth estate and that the pen is mightier than the sword. In an exquisitely inexact and unpredictable way, there is power in a few of these words that we write, but it's a fickle power resembling the priest's prayer for rain. Sometimes he gets it and sometimes he doesn't, but even when he does it may not come the way he wants it. He may get flooded out.[3]

In any case, however fickle it may be, power represents one of the reasons why the media of mass communication deal in the opinion business.

The proprietors of the press, whether the Greeleys and Pulitzers of a bygone day or the Sulzbergers (*New York Times*), the Stantons (CBS), and the von Hoffmans of the present, have found the control of great engines of information and influence a gratifying challenge.

Down through the generations, some of the controllers of the media of information have used their leverage to support political candidacies for themselves or for others, to ventilate their personal prejudices, to build up profitable media empires, or to better the lot of the public. The opinion function has represented one of the most significant ways in which this leverage has been applied. And it still does today.

BUT NOT ONLY POWER

Yet the power it affords is not the only reason—often not even the chief reason—why the editors, the managers, and the owners of the media of mass communication regard the opinion function as important.

Many of them feel that the space or time their publication or network can devote to thoughtful analysis represents a kind of showcase effort, a counterbalance to the sometimes shallow, routine, or trivial matter that takes up much of the rest of the space in the newspaper or the time on the broadcaster's program schedule. They are able, in the editorial section of the paper or on the TV documentary special, to offer a quality of writing and a level of production that cannot be managed easily within the tight deadlines of the newspaper operation or in the face of the lowest-common-denominator pressures that bear on the TV programmer.

One newspaper editor, Robert McCord of the *Little Rock* (Ark.) *Democrat*, describes the editorial page as the newspaper's personality and adds that none of us would want to invite into our homes people without personalities.

Louis M. Lyons, former curator of the Nieman Foundation at Harvard University, once told a meeting of newspaper editorial writers:

> If one needed an excuse for an editorial page, or to try to define the primary role of the page, I think it would be to express the tone of the paper. This, even more than the policy of the paper. It's a chance to represent the institution itself, as a civilized and civilizing force, as a concerned and considerate citizen, as a moderate and moderating influence, as a thoughtful person, a good neighbor, one who cares. The tone reflects the character of

the paper. Whatever else, whatever encroachments, this remains your charge. Some would think it is enough. I hope you do.[4]

The TV executive, too, hopes that his institution's tone will be seen in the hour-long examination in depth of a national problem, rather than in the soap opera interlude of midday, or the succession of sit-com slots in prime time.

THE GYROSCOPE FUNCTION

Lyons's observation alluded in passing to a third reason why the mass media lay stress on (and spend money on) the opinion function. He spoke of the editorial page as a "civilizing force," a "moderating influence." Others have talked of the *gyroscope function* that the editorial page and its counterparts in broadcasting and magazines serve for society in general. A eulogist at the funeral of a famed editor said that the state had lost its "rudder and compass." All of these comments were referring to the contribution the media of information can make by bringing meaning out of the jumble of news and events and by keeping in view the central values of our age despite the tides of passion and propaganda that swirl about and obscure them.

However you label it, the gyroscope function is profoundly important. And it is one that is not carried out by very many elements of our society. Political, union, or industrial leaders usually are case makers for their own vested interests. The stabilizing institutions of the past, the church and the school, are devalued today. Scholar Daniel Bell put the plight of modern man in mass society graphically:

> The old primary group ties of family and local community have been shattered; ancient parochial faiths are questioned; few unifying values have taken their place. Most important, the critical standards of an educated elite no longer shape opinion or taste. As a result, mores and morals are in constant flux, relations between individuals are tangential or compartmentalized rather than organic. At the same time greater mobility, spatial and social, intensifies concern over status. Instead of a fixed or known status, symbolized by dress or title, each person assumes a multiplicity of roles and constantly has to prove himself in a succession of new situations. Because of all this, the individual loses a coherent sense of self. His anxieties increase. There ensues a search for new faiths. The stage is thus set for the charismatic leader, the secular messiah, who, by bestowing on each person the semblance

of necessary grace and fullness of personality, supplies a substitute for the older undying belief that mass society has destroyed.[5]

The analysts of the mass media, if they are trusted and if they do their job well, can help to restore at least some balance and stability to the frightening scene Bell sketches. By helping to explain the significance of the glut of events, by sorting out issues at stake, the practitioners of the editorial function can help the reader or viewer to avoid being drowned in the mass society. By calling attention to the ways in which central values of our system are being endangered, they can counter the appeal of the glib demagogue with the "simple" answers.

From time to time, the editorial writers and analysts have risen to this kind of challenge. During the early 1950s the mood of the American public was uneasy and worried; our atomic monopoly was gone, and we were naked in the world. And there was Sen. Joseph R. McCarthy, bringing us fearful news about Communists infiltrating our government and threatening the national security. He caught the wave of national hysteria and rode it dramatically, denouncing public servants and national leaders on the flimsiest of evidence or no evidence at all.

Someone had to say "Hold, wait—there may be some problem here, but let's not burn the house down to save it." Although they were somewhat belated in recognizing their responsibilities, the editorial writers and the broadcasters (notably Murrow of CBS) did step forward to point out that the demagogic senator was effectively destroying the liberties of Americans while professing to be defending them. And they thus contributed materially to calming the national mood and discrediting the McCarthy tactics.

A few years later, Sen. Estes Kefauver's hearings into corruption and crime brought a parade of mobsters to the witness stand. One after another, they claimed the protection of the Fifth Amendment to the Constitution (prohibiting enforced self-incrimination). A public outcry arose for repeal of this pesky shield for hoodlums. Again, editorial writers and others tried to bring the matter back into perspective, pointing out that the protection against self-incrimination was a right vital to all of us, one of the cornerstones of our legal system, and not to be sacrificed in a mood of exasperation because it was being used by a few unlovely lawbreakers.

More recently, when dissenters against the continuing war in Vietnam incurred the wrath of sizable groups of citizens and were branded traitors, it was necessary for someone to come forward with the reminder that truly basic values were involved, that the right to dissent is an integral part of a democratic society. Some editors and commentators, though not all by any means, did make that contribution.

These kinds of efforts to bring the national discussion back to basics— to act as gyroscope—represent an exceedingly important aspect of the opinion function in the mass media. And to many of the men who manage the media, this is the most compelling reason for continuing to emphasize the opinion function. Barry Bingham, editor and publisher (also president and owner) of the *Louisville Courier-Journal,* points out:

> I spend at least half of my own time by choice working directly on an editorial page, because I like the work and because I believe deeply in its usefulness. It is my settled conviction that the editorial page is the heart and soul of a good newspaper. It can also be the conscience of the newspaper, and to an important degree, the conscience of the community in which it is published.[6]

The last few pages have detailed some of the values of the opinion function as seen by the men who wield it through the media of mass communication. But what of its value to the consumer, the presumed beneficiary of all this effort? What purposes do the editorialists and the analysts serve for him?

BENEFITS RECOGNIZED AND UNRECOGNIZED

One of the values of the opinion function of the mass media from the consumer's viewpoint is, of course, the gyroscope influence. The reader or viewer may not often (or ever) be conscious of this as a benefit to him, but clearly it is. There are other values for him in the opinion function, and of these he is more often aware.

First, he seeks from the mass media, and often gets, an *explanation* of the "blooming, buzzing confusion" around him. So much of the news in this complex era is simply not understandable on its face. What can the reader or viewer make of an announcement that the gross national product will shortly approach the $1,200 billion mark? Or of an assertion by a senator that unless we deploy a whole new family of anti-ballistic missiles we shall be helplessly vulnerable to a nuclear Pearl Harbor? Or of the news that drug addiction will soon be as prevalent in the cool, green, affluent suburbs as in the inner-city jungles?

Piling on more and more information, more facts, may not help at all to clarify the meaning of these and the thousands of similar developments that make up the mosaic of the news on any given day. As was noted in Chapter 1, simply providing more information may stifle rather than enhance understanding. What the man in the street sorely needs are the services of people who can sift through the flow of events and interpret them, give them meaning in human terms—and who do *not* have some special interest to serve. He turns consciously to the various mass media for that kind of service, and he frequently gets it from the opinion function of those media.

Second, but perhaps less consciously, he turns to the opinion framers for another kind of help. He looks for *bench marks* against which to test his own thinking and shape his own conclusions about the meaning of events.

Most of us don't reason our way through to conclusions with the clear precision of the logicians. We are more apt to mull an issue over, shifting now this way, now that, as evidence or viewpoints come to our attention. Often an opinion will develop in vague, embryonic form, but stay in the background of the mind, unready to come out in the open.

In such circumstances there is value in encountering someone else's firmly argued viewpoint. It may be one that accords generally with the line of reasoning toward which we were groping in the background of the mind; if so, it may channel (or, as communication theorists put it, *canalize*) our thinking another stage along the way to conviction.

But the outside argument can be equally valuable if it runs sharply counter to our own half-formed viewpoint. By providing us with something firm and solid against which to thrust our own arguments, the opposing view may perform a catalytic function, and we may begin to grasp more clearly the position that we shall finally adopt.

Those who work at the opinion function of the mass media—the editorial writer, the TV commentator, the magazine essayist, the syndicated columnist—typically neither seek nor get a knee-jerk, obedient following. But they do contribute materially to their readers and viewers by facilitating the thinking process and providing the kind of catalysts that help turn amorphous leanings into recognizable convictions.

TALKING BACK

The opinion sections of the mass media provide a third benefit to the consumer, one that is certainly as important as the other two. They constitute a *public forum,* just about the last one available to the average citizen in the present-day world. One of the most frustrating aspects of the mass society that Daniel Bell described is the awesome immensity of it so far as the individual is concerned. There are so few opportunities to make a mark, register a protest, or get a hearing before one's fellows.

In simpler societies the individual often counted for more in many respects. He had a say in the deliberations of his community—in the forum of the ancient city-states, or at the annual town meeting in colonial American villages. But in today's society, unless he has vast funds at his disposal to buy a hearing through advertising space or time, the average citizen is virtually voiceless: except, that is, for the opportunities afforded him by the mailbags, letters sections, or talk shows of the media of mass communication.

There he has a fair-to-middling chance to air his opinions, protests, or proposals and be reasonably sure that a sizable number of his fellow citizens will become aware of them. In the small newspaper or on the small-market radio or TV station, the odds are very good; most letters to the editor are published, if they aren't obscene or legally actionable, and most callers can be accommodated on the community talk shows. The chances that his particular contribution will be accepted by a metropolitan newspaper or the letters section of *Time* or *Newsweek* are far smaller, but they are not hopeless by any means.

The editors at all levels treat the letters from readers as an important component of the opinion function—and they are right in their judgment. The contributions from the audience represent a needed safety valve, an opening for diversity of viewpoint, and a blessed chance for the individual to speak up to the world through a mighty megaphone and be heard—if only for a brief moment. Life in the mass society would be even less palatable than it is without that chance.

NOTES

1. By reiterating in his editorials the slogan "On to Richmond!" Greeley pressured the government into undertaking the first battle of Bull Run, a premature and disastrous venture as it turned out. Greeley later sought to disclaim responsibility, but he was generally assigned the credit (or blame).

2. Historians do not agree about the degree of influence the two editors exerted on the movement toward war. Locked in a circulation battle, Pulitzer and Hearst were striving to out-sensationalize each other, and the Cuban situation was made to order for their purposes. They undoubtedly fanned the national mood into belligerency, but it

would not be realistic to charge them with creating the Spanish-American War from a cold start.

3. Nicholas von Hoffman, quoted in *Masthead*, Spring 1971, p. 41.

4. From a speech delivered by Louis M. Lyons to the annual meeting of the National Conference of Editorial Writers at Boston, October 2, 1970.

5. Daniel Bell, "The Theory of Mass Society," *Commentary*, July 1956, p. 75.

6. In a speech at MacMurray College, Jacksonville, Illinois, on February 17, 1962.

3
Two Facts of Life

Before this exploration of the opinion function proceeds any further, there are two facts of life that need to be discussed—and discussed explicitly, not in coy birds-and-bees terms.

One of these has to do with the intellectual equipment of the editorial writer, columnist, or commentator; the other concerns the degree of freedom the opinion writer has to ventilate his own viewpoints. Let's turn first to the matter of intellectual equipment.

Newcomers to the field of opinion writing very often have the misconception that their role is largely one of surface skills: mastery of a repertoire of rhetoric and of the technology of persuasion. They do need to have or to acquire such mastery, to be sure. But if that is all they have to offer they have no business hanging out their shingles as editorial writers.

Consider for a moment, in the light of the discussion in the last chapter, what role the opinion writer fills. He is combination *philosopher, historian, advocate,* and *educator.* He must somehow lift himself above partisan involvements to take a long view of the events that crowd in heated confusion, just as the judge on the bench must take himself out of the spirit of the adversary proceedings and the courtroom theatrics when he attempts to balance the scales.

For his multi-hat function, the opinion writer needs more than the ability to write ably and to organize an argument with a sure sense of logic. He needs to *know something substantive,* preferably a good many substantive somethings.

He must be an educated person, in the most catholic sense of that term. He need not be a da Vinci, a Renaissance man, but he must—he *must*—have a solid fund of knowledge on which to base his analyses, predictions, and advocacies.

NO WOODEN NICKELS NEEDED

Empty, top-of-the-head opinions are the cheapest currency of the intellectual marketplace. The opinion function of the mass media must offer better coin than that. Otherwise it deserves to go out of business—and it will.

Edward C. Banfield, a Harvard professor and author of *The Un-Heavenly City,* addressed himself to a group of newspaper editors in these words:

> It would take a gifted man weeks, months, or even years to do a really serious investigation and analysis of most of the subjects—several of them a day—on which the newspaper is expected to pronounce every morning or every evening. How many subscribers would be willing to pay the several dollars a day that it would cost for a paper written by people who had studied every subject profoundly and could write about it lucidly and entertainingly? Probably few readers would take such a paper even if it were free. Not many people are prepared to face the consequences of a serious inquiry into a problem, for it almost always turns out that the problem has no solution—a finding that is likely to be frustrating and anxiety-provoking. Just as good news sells more papers than bad, so, I suspect, "solutions" that do not challenge "what everybody knows" sell more newspapers than do dilemmas and hard choices derived from unfamiliar and therefore unplausible premises.[1]

Banfield's lack of familiarity with the newspaper field leads him a bit astray (e.g., it is "bad" news that sells newspapers rather than "good" news), and in his description of the ideal news analysis he is talking in terms of the kind of scholarly discourse that would be more appropriate to a textbook on international relations than to a newspaper or magazine. But there is an essential truth in his comment, nevertheless.

That truth is his insistence that solid knowledge must lie behind analysis if that analysis is to be of any value for those to whom it is directed.

The opinion writer cannot be a universal genius; not even Professor Banfield would ask that. But he can be thoroughly grounded in one field (economics, say, or government, or urban sociology) or several and be conversant with a good many more. His life necessarily must be a prolonged educational experience; for him, four years on campus and the routine B.A. are nowhere near enough.[2] He must go on learning as long as he goes on writing, and ideally he ought to continue learning not only on his own initiative but through periodic refresher visits to academe. Such returns have become increasingly feasible in recent years with the institution of such back-to-campus sabbatical programs as that of the Nieman Foundation at Harvard, the Professional Journalism Fellowships at Stanford, and the Urban Journalism Center at Northwestern University. These programs are aimed not at refurbishing journalistic skills but at enabling working newsmen to dig into substantive academic areas they need to know about if they are to function effectively in their jobs once they get back to the desk a year or six months later.

Anyone contemplating a career as an opinion writer ought to be very clear at the outset about this fact of life in the field. He must *know* something before he can counsel or educate or advocate; if he has nothing more to offer than a facile way with the typewriter and the language, he's a fraud from the start and it won't take long for his audience to find him out.

WHOSE SOAPBOX?

A second common misconception of the neophyte wielder of the opinion function is that now he is free of institutional restraints and craft conventions; now he can sound off from a personal platform and let the world share his undiluted wisdom. But unless he is in a very special situation, he rapidly discovers that this notion runs counter to another fact of life: Most opinion writers are not totally free agents. They don't have full title to the soapbox.

There are a few, of course, who are indeed in that happy position. They are those who are both editorial writers and owners (Barry Bingham of Louisville is one) or others who are in a sense freelancers, entrepreneurs who are good enough to command a following independent of any specific media vehicle (syndicated columnists or cartoonists, for example). But even these latter are usually based on some paper (columnist James Reston works for the *New York Times,* which syndicates his column, and cartoonist Herblock has his home base at the *Washington Post*) and thus must fit within the policy context of that institution to at least some degree.

And most opinion writers definitely operate within a framework, a context not determined only by them. They enunciate policy positions that are those of a magazine, a newspaper, or a network—not just their personal views.

To be sure, if they are associated with enlightened publications that value their role as analysts, they may have a very wide latitude in the formation of editorial policy. But that latitude is typically shared with an editorial board or conference of some kind, particularly on larger publications, so there still isn't one-man rule.

Sometimes the boundaries within which the opinion writer has freedom to operate are so wide-flung that he rarely runs any risk of colliding with them. But he is always aware that they exist. One editorial writer put it explicitly:

> The most independent among us, who labor under the most amiable and enlightened editors, and who roam almost unchecked over the entire spectrum of social and political commentary, are nonetheless faced with boundaries that may not be crossed, however tempting the view from the far side. . . . Thus, however much an editorial writer is persuaded that a collectivist economy controlled by the state is the only solution to such problems as poverty, health care, pollution, he may not advocate the dissolution of the so-called free enterprise system. An *a priori* premise in all our social commentary is that the American system is uniquely fitted to usher in the age of abundance for all. That it does not do so is evidence that the system needs to be modified, adjusted, improved (or left totally alone); but the principles of the system are sound.[3]

Let's note again that the opinion writer, on whatever medium, often has a very great deal to say about the policy context within which he functions. He typically has a fuller freedom to shape policy than the reader or viewer supposes. But he almost never has *absolute* freedom, and the prospective opinion writer who has such a gleam in his eye had better moderate it, unless he has a spare $10 million or so to buy his own media soapbox or unless he commands enough genius to achieve a following independent of any journalistic home base.

NOTES

1. Edward C. Banfield, "Are You Part of the Problem or Part of the Solution?" *Bulletin of the American Society of Newspaper Editors,* July–August 1970, p. 12.

2. The author, when working as an editorial writer specializing in economic news, was expected to keep abreast on a daily basis with the two papers for which he worked (a morning-evening metropolitan combination), the *New York Times,* the *New York Herald Tribune,* the *Wall Street Journal,* the *Times* (London), and the Manchester *Guardian.* He was also expected to be up-to-date on numerous periodicals that

crossed his desk, including the *Federal Reserve Bulletin,* the *Economist,* the *Monthly Labor Review,* various bank letters, publications of the Committee for Economic Development, and numerous business and trade weeklies and monthlies. All of this required daily allocation of reading or study time considerably in excess of that of the typical undergraduate—or graduate student, for that matter.

3. Harold Piety, editorial writer of the *Dayton* (Ohio) *Journal Herald,* in "Tools of the Interests? Of Course We Are!" *Masthead,* Spring 1970, pp. 13–14.

4
Who Says What, and Why, and to Whom?

The policy framework within which opinion writers function on a newspaper, magazine, or broadcasting station is not often formally written down somewhere, on a charter, a guidebook, or tablets of stone. It is more typically a viewpoint generally understood within the shop, a philosophy that is part of the atmosphere and that permeates the woodwork.

To be sure, there are some publications that post a slogan on the masthead that speaks in general terms of the policy followed by their writers and editors. The *St. Louis Post-Dispatch,* for example, includes on its editorial page each day the following valedictory from its founder, which first appeared on April 10, 1907:

The *Post-Dispatch* Platform

I know that my retirement will make no difference in its cardinal principles. That it will always fight for progress and reform, never tolerate injustice or corruption, always fight demagogues of all parties, never belong to any party, always oppose privileged classes and public plunderers, never lack sympathy with the poor, always remain devoted to the public welfare, never be satisfied with merely printing news, always be drastically independent, never be afraid to attack wrong, whether by predatory plutocracy or predatory poverty.—Joseph Pulitzer

Such lofty and unexceptionable statements may serve as philosophical umbrellas for publications. But as a practical matter, policy tends to be worked out on an issue-by-issue basis somewhere within the broad range of territory covered by such an umbrella.

On the very small publication, the development of policy is likely to be a short and simple matter. The editor (who is often also the publisher, owner, reporter, and advertising director) faces up to the office mirror, confers briefly, and then decides whether the *Bugle* that day will come out for or against the urgent issue of the moment.

If the publication is a very small one—say a community weekly—it may not come out for or against *anything*. The hard-pressed small-town editor or broadcast station manager simply has so many other things to do that he cannot devote much time to mulling over the problems of the times and inditing thoughtful explanations and resolutions of them.

And that is unfortunate, since the small-town editor often has useful insights to share with his readers. Admittedly, he may not be any better posted on world or national events than are his subscribers. But in all probability he *does* know his community and its problems better than anyone else in town, since this is his full-time occupation. If he could find the time—and if he were willing to take the risks—he could contribute meaningfully to the discussion of community issues.

That phrase, "if he were willing to take the risks," has a special meaning for the small-town opinion writer. Community newspapers and broadcasting stations are far more vulnerable to the pressures of advertisers or other special interests than are their big-city counterparts, which are virtually immune to such pressures by virtue of their monopoly or semimonopoly situation.

An editor who steps on sensitive toes in a small town may find himself facing a potentially ruinous boycott or an imported competitor financed by his enemies. The awareness of such threats in the background has led some small-town editors to give up the opinion function altogether or else concern themselves only with safe and distant topics (about which the writers usually do not have much to say, since they can't take the time to be deeply informed).

This does not have to be the case, and in fact it is not the case in some fortunate small towns. The community of Clinton, New York, for example, has, in its weekly *Courier,* an opinion page that is neither mealymouthed nor plagued by Afghanistanism (comment prudently aimed at far-off targets with no local ties).

The *Courier's* editor, Jack Boynton, thinks editorials are as important on a weekly as on a daily, and he writes 90 percent of his editorials on local subjects. In 1969 he was quoted as estimating that "in 13 years, I've written something like 2,000 editorials. Obviously some are repetitive, but the approach is usually fresh—not contradictory unless events lead to a change in my stand. That's happened. No editorial writer should be inflexible."[1] Boynton writes about three editorials an issue, as well as an editor's column in a light vein. He doesn't believe in avoiding issues or stands. "To surround a subject without taking some sort of stand is to do a half-job."

There have been others who have proved—sometimes at cost to themselves—that small-town opinion writing does not have to be characterized by blandness, timidity, and Afghanistanism. Among them was Hazel Brannon Smith, who won the Pulitzer Prize in 1964 for her editorials in the *Lexington Advertiser,* a tiny Mississippi weekly, in which she battled against the segregationist White Citizens Councils in her state. There was also Edward L. Geymann, editor and publisher of the *Western Butler County Times* of Towanda, Kansas, who used his editorial page to combat the issue of religious bigotry when it was introduced during the 1960 presidential campaign. And there was Samuel L. Woodring, editor of the *North Augusta* (S.C.) *Star,* who fought to weed out incompetence and corruption from the local police force, despite organized advertising boycotts and physical assaults on both the editor and members of his family.

The fact remains, however, that it takes an unusually gifted individual, and one with uncommon courage, to conduct the opinion function in a one-man situation. Many small-town editors have abdicated the responsibility.

OUT ON THE TABLE

If you turn from small publications to the larger ones, the determination of editorial policy becomes increasingly complex; it's no longer simply a matter of the editor and his mirror agreeing.

There may be several editorial writers, the editor or publisher (or both), possibly a cartoonist, and one or two other functionaries involved in the policy-setting process. Usually, the larger the publication the more elaborate the staff involved in fashioning the opinion section. The *New York Times* has perhaps the largest editorial section staff of any newspaper (ten editorial writers, plus several editors), but many smaller papers also devote surprisingly substantial resources to the editorial page. As an instance, the *Eugene* (Oreg.) *Register-Guard,* a daily of 55,000 circulation, has three full-time editorial writers.

When from a half dozen to a dozen persons may be involved in some fashion in setting the policy of a publication on the issues of the day, there usually has to be some structured forum to facilitate the hammering-out process. On many metropolitan newspapers and some magazines, this takes the form of the *editorial conference.*

The author was for a number of years a member of such a conference. A description of its operation may provide a fairly typical picture of the way in which editorial policies are developed on large newspapers.[2] The conference would convene daily, at mid-morning. The editorial writers would have spent the first part of the morning reading through the local papers as well as those from other eastern cities and some from abroad. Each of the writers had an area of specialization (state and local government, international affairs, economics) and would have been scanning the news for topics that fell within his area of responsibility.

Each might also have spent some of the morning checking into the technical periodicals in his field for additional background on some issue in the day's news columns. All the writers would have worked out in rough outline an idea or two for editorials that might be written later that day for publication in the next morning's paper.

When the conference assembled around the table in the editorial library, there would be the six editorial writers (one of them the chief editorial writer, or editorial page editor as he is termed on some publications), the editor of the paper, one or both of the two editorial cartoonists, the editor of the Sunday survey-of-the-week section, and the managing editor of the afternoon paper, who was on hand to provide a last-minute summary of the wire-service reports just in.

As the conference got under way, one writer would sketch out a treatment he proposed to give a topic in the news. Other members of the conference would react—sometimes objecting to the suggested line of argument, sometimes supplying additional points, sometimes cautioning against a built-in weakness in the reasoning. The give-and-take would be brisk, efficient, and sometimes blunt or heated. Usually, as the exchange developed, a consensus would jell. It might be in support of the original idea or it might form on quite a different theme. If the conference turned out to be split and no consensus could be reached, whoever was presiding (the editor, if he were on hand, the chief editorial writer otherwise) would resolve the matter and determine which stand would be taken. Then another of the writers would lay his brainchild of the morning on the table and the whole process would be repeated.

By the time the conference adjourned an hour or two later, anywhere from half a dozen to a dozen full-fledged editorial topics would have been worked over and approved. The writers would then scatter to their individual offices to write the pieces, some of them to be turned in to the chief editorial writer later in the day for editing; those requiring more extended time for research were not expected for another day or even several days.

Usually the editorial writer who had first advanced a topic would be the one to write the piece. But if his original proposal had been materially revised or even reversed in the discussion phase, he might no longer want to work on it. In that case, someone else on the board who did agree with the consensus theme would take it over. No writer was ever asked to write an editorial with which he could not agree. This policy was not only in deference to the sensibilities of the writers; it also had a practical side. A writer who is lukewarm on a topic—or even stone cold—is not likely to do a very thorough or persuasive job with it. The end result may be so halting and illformed that the only sensible thing to do is to put it out of its misery; to publish it would be to waste the space.

WARTS AND ALL

The conference system of formulating editorial policy has one notable virtue. It provides a means of giving a proposed editorial idea a rugged road test before it is sent out into the world.

By the time a topic has been worked over by a half dozen well-posted editors, all of them schooled to argumentation and research, its warts and flaws will have been identified. Holes in the fabric of reasoning will have been spotted and stitched over. Omissions that would have been painfully embarrassing had they gone into print will have been noted and the necessary additions made.

An editorial writer sitting alone in his office, building an editorial theme from start to final draft, can easily become so bemused by his own brilliant eloquence and overpowering logic that he fails to notice that one corner of his dream castle is resting on sand or that he forgot to put in any stairways. Any piece of writing can benefit from the searching scrutiny of others, and this is particularly true of opinion writing. Case making, whether for print or broadcast, must be done with precision and utmost care if it is to have any impact. If the writer leaves any handhold for the hostile or skeptical among the audience to grasp—an egregious error, a glaring nonsequitur—the whole structure can be overturned in a moment and all the effort wasted.

This testing process, which helps to make certain that the editorial will stand up to critical appraisal, is the great advantage of the conference approach. Some small-town editors who have no colleagues to constitute a conference attempt to achieve some of the same results by trying editorial ideas out in advance on individual members of the community—"field testing," one midwestern editor calls it.

LOSING THE EDGE

There are drawbacks to the conference method, which somewhat counterbalance that one substantial advantage.

For one thing, any project undertaken by committee is very likely to turn out to be a structure of compromise. An idea that comes to the table in sharply etched form, an incisive and pointed theme, may emerge from the pull and tug of discussion half an hour later with its edge gone. So many "yes, but" provisions will have been worked into it, so many contingencies allowed for, that the thrust of the original proposal will have been blunted and softened. The finished piece may have a cautiously corporate flavor. It may be tight enough and secure from critical attack on technical or logical grounds. But it may also be a good deal duller than the piece the writer had originally had in mind.

A second problem arises from the fact that, if a publication is large enough to have enough manpower for an editorial conference, it very likely is also the case that the writers who make up the conference are all specialists in some field. Each of them knows his own intellectual bailiwick intimately; he may be far less well informed about the next man's territory. Thus when an issue—say, of welfare policy—comes up, the expert in that field can spin out a persuasive and authoritative line of argument; his colleagues may seek to spot holes in it, but they are at a disadvantage since they are nowhere near as familiar with the subject as he is. So the rugged testing that theoretically takes place in the conference may not amount to much in this instance. Nor may it work out any better when the next expert's turn comes to sketch out an idea in his own area of expertise.

A newspaper reporter who formerly had been an editorial writer has written of what lies behind the "myth of editorial policy":

> On all but a few truly major items (what presidential candidate to support, whether to back or oppose the war in Viet Nam) editorials in American newspapers are the product of the personal opinion or judgment of one man. . . . The whole system works

that way. The man is hired for good reason as capable or even expert in a field and as generally in sympathy with the orientation of the paper (insofar as that can be determined). He reads thoroughly in this subject. He goes to the morning editorial conference and proposes an editorial in his field. There is desultory, and necessarily brief, discussion of what he suggests. The editorial board chief then may make a decision or two about which subjects to write about at all.

But after the conference breaks up, our man knows only that he is to write the subject he brought up. The rest is entirely up to him. Barring a major challenge by the editorial board chief (himself, of course, merely an individual with individual opinions), what he writes appears as it is.[3]

That picture is a bit out of focus so far as many editorial conferences are concerned, but there is undoubtedly some truth in it. The disadvantages inherent in the conference system do not, for most large papers, outweigh the one important advantage discussed earlier. The system continues to be used widely. But there are some papers with substantial editorial staffs that forego the approach. The *New York Times* does not hold a regular conference; the editorial page editor talks individually with the various writers and later looks over the work they produce before sending it to the composing room.

Other publications use a variation on the traditional conference, convening the editorial page staff for luncheon meetings, frequently with important visitors as guest resource persons (the *Boston Herald* and the *St. Louis Post-Dispatch* have tried this tack). But if the discussions at these luncheon sessions are as freewheeling as at other editorial conferences, the incidence of heartburn later in the day must be impressive.

WHO CALLS THE SHOTS?

The foregoing examination of the mechanics of editorial policy formulation did not deal with the important matter of *why* a given policy stand is chosen. It's a good deal easier, of course, to describe the *how*. Getting at the reasons why Paper X supports Policy A calls for a probing of motives, conscious and subconscious, a penetration of the editorial sanctum to see what values weigh on the scales as the publication's policy makers go about their business.

Many consumers of the opinion product of the various mass media apparently think they know what influences are decisive; the layman, if asked, will say that it is of course the big advertiser and the publication's owners who call the shots.

The author once put some questions about newspaper editorial policy making to a sizable sample of readers in four Oregon communities; 466 persons chosen by random selection were questioned by trained interviewers. The respondents were readers of eight different papers: local weeklies or dailies and regional dailies; nearly all of the respondents were regular readers of more than one.

One of the questions asked was, "Which of the following, if any, do you think would be likely to influence the editorial page opinion of the newspaper on a controversial issue?" The figures in the table indicate the percentage of the respondents who identified each category as likely to be influential.[4] The views of

editorial writers	45%
politicians	40%
business and industrial leaders	37%
letters-to-the-editor writers	33%
the owners	31%
labor union leaders	28%
advertisers	27%
clergy	25%
police	24%
teachers and professors	23%
don't know	12%

The findings must have been somewhat humbling for the editorial writers on the eight papers involved, since only 45 percent of the respondents believed that the writers were influential in shaping the policies their pages espoused. Most of the other figures were predictable—particularly those indicating the respondents' impression that the publications' owners, local businessmen, and advertisers had a good deal to say about policy stands. The degree of influence attributed to writers of letters to the editor was surprising, at least to the conductor of the survey; it might in part be explained by the fact that from time to time editorials are written in response to, or in supplement to, a letter from a reader. This may mistakenly convey the impression that letter writers affect editorial policy.

But how well-founded are the public's impressions about the leverage that these various groups are able to exert on the newspaper's policy setters?

SOME MISCONCEPTIONS

To begin with, the public considerably underestimates the role of the editorial writers themselves as shapers of policy. On most papers, the members of the editorial board play a major part, individually and collectively, in determining what issues will be taken up and what positions advanced.

In so doing, they of course reflect the varied and complex factors that have gone into the gradual development of their own personal frames of reference. These frames of reference vary from individual to individual, and their interaction on a given editorial page staff might shift and tilt from day to day in almost kaleidoscopic fashion.

Cataloging the individual biases of opinion writers would be impossible and pointless, but it might be worth noting some of the generalized conclusions of a study, "A Profile of the Editorial Writer," conducted by two educators at Indiana University, Cleveland Wilhoit and Dan Drew.[5]

They drew their profile based on the responses of 372 editorial writers who were active in the field in 1971. Among their findings were these:

- Nearly all of the editorial writers responding (82.8 percent) were college graduates, and more than 20 percent had at least one advanced degree.
- In response to the question "As of today, which of the following best describes your political leanings?" the editorial writers indicated the following ideological breakdown:

Political leanings	Per Cent
Democrat	30.54
Republican	17.07
Independent	48.20
Independent Republican	.90
Independent Democrat	.30
Other	2.99

- More than 66 percent of the respondents indicated that their editor discouraged public participation in politics by editorial writers, and most of the writers indicated agreement with this view—at least insofar as it involved membership in partisan political organizations. But 42 percent of the respondents reported that they did engage in some form of political activity beyond voting—by contributing money, attending political rallies, or writing a candidate's speeches.

■ About one-third of the respondents said that they belonged to no public affairs organizations, presumably to avoid any influence such membership might exert on them in their policy-making role. However, 45 percent indicated that they held membership in civic, religious, fraternal, or veterans groups; 30.5 percent said they were members of the boards of nonprofit organizations; and a little more than 10 percent of the total said they held membership on district, municipal, or state boards and agencies.

All of these factors play their part, in varying degrees on various issues, as the editorial writers approach their daily tasks of fashioning the publication's policy. Yet the paper's readers are not likely to be conscious of this influence on editorial policy; in some respects, the readers' impressions, if they do have any, are likely to be erroneous. For example, the profile's findings on the political leanings of editorial writers would probably surprise most readers.

THOSE SINISTER "INTERESTS"

There are also misconceptions in the public view about the influence that big advertisers or other special-interest groups can wield. Except for the special case of the very small community paper noted earlier, most newspapers are relatively invulnerable to outside pressures. And most broadcasters try to keep the news and opinion sectors of their program schedule free of such pressures, even though they of course pay a great deal of attention to advertisers' views so far as the entertainment content of their medium is concerned.

Nor do politicians or public officials swing much weight in the editorial conferences. Their views and actions are frequently the subject of editorial comment, to be sure, but they have little success if they try to dictate a publication's news or editorial policy. The *New York Times* and *Washington Post* underlined this point dramatically when, in 1971, they defied the full panoply of the federal government—the White House, the Justice Department, even court injunctions—and pressed ahead with the publication of the secret Pentagon Papers detailing how this country entangled its armed forces in the Vietnam War.

But if these factors are not the determining ones when an editorial policy is being shaped, which considerations *do* count? Who—or what— really calls the shots?

Obviously, there can be no blanket answer to these questions. And, equally obviously, any attempt to make a sure identification of the determinants of policy on any given publication would require putting the policy makers on a psychiatrist's couch for a thorough probing. So we must make do with outcroppings of evidence here and there and some reasonably well-informed speculation. What follows should be taken in that spirit.

THEY SIGN THE CHECKS

One influence certainly is that of ownership. On that part of the survey question, the 466 Oregon respondents had the right notion.

But the degree to which ownership representatives hand down dicta to the editorial writers varies considerably from publication to publication.

In earlier days (when the elder Hearst still ruled from San Simeon, or when Col. Robert McCormick of the *Chicago Tribune* was alive) editorial writers sometimes were only megaphones or conduits for the transmission of the biases and whims of ownership. That condition persists today in some individual newspapers, magazines, or broadcasting stations. But oftener than the layman might suppose, the owners keep hands off and let the experts they have hired to wield the opinion function have relatively free rein.

On almost any medium of mass communication there will be some issues so cosmic that even a hands-off ownership will want to have the final say. A survey of editorial writers conducted by *Masthead,* the quarterly publication of the National Conference of Editorial Writers, after the 1964 presidential election made it plain that, in the vast majority of cases, the decision as to whether the paper would back Johnson or Goldwater was one that came down from the front office.[6] But not many issues are as momentous.

The publisher of the *New York Times,* Arthur Ochs Sulzberger, told an interviewer that it is the editorial page editor, John Oakes, and his staff who set the policy for that journal. "John calls the shots for most of the editorials," Sulzberger said. "On the rare occasion we have fudged a little, debated it back and forth, and arrived at a middle ground with which we could both live. This is very rare. Once in every eight, nine, or ten months."[7]

The impression conveyed by the *Times* publisher is a bit misleading, however. Oakes may indeed be largely free of the direct influence of the publisher; but Oakes himself is a member of the *Times*'s ruling family, a descendant of the Adolph Ochs who came up from Chattanooga to make the paper the national institution it is today. Oakes may hold little *Times* stock, but he is not exactly a hired hand, either.

Other bits of evidence like the Sulzberger interview come to light now and then to suggest the kinds of relationships that exist between ownership and opinion writers. During one gubernatorial election campaign in New York, for example, the *New York Post* came out editorially in support of the candidacy of Democrat Averell Harriman. Its stand was written and signed by the editor, Jimmy Wechsler. But on the front page there appeared a second editorial endorsement, this one of Republican Nelson Rockefeller, and the writer was the paper's owner, Mrs. Dorothy Schiff. Presumably Mrs. Schiff could have used her position to order the editor to take the stand she wanted; she chose instead the other course.

On some newspaper chains and on some broadcasting networks, opinion pieces are written at a central headquarters and then used by all the components of the chain or network, word for word. On other group or chain operations, a wide degree of local autonomy is evident (some of the papers in the Newhouse chain regularly support Democrats, others are as consistently Republican).

So the picture is a mixed one. There is always the potentiality of ownership intervention in policy formation; often it does not take place in a direct sense. Yet any candid assessment of the situation would also have to take into account the "elevator syndrome"—the osmotic transfer of the publisher's opinions and biases to his editorial writers as they ride up and down the office elevator or have other informal associations. Ownership may not have to take a direct hand at the conference table very often; the writers may have divined the viewpoint of the directors and reflect it without being ordered to.

Candor would also require that we note that, when there is policy dictation by outside ownership (that is, ownership not directly involved in the day-to-day operation of the publication as are such owner-publishers as Barry Bingham at the *Louisville Courier-Journal,* Sulzberger at the *Times,* or Otis Chandler at the *Los Angeles Times*), the results are very likely to be unhappy. Herbert Brucker, himself a former editor (*Hartford Courant*) and later director of the Professional Journalism Fellowship Program at Stanford, sketched the possibilities pungently:

> There is, of course, a reason why a businessman in command of a paper pulls his editors' punches. For one thing, an editorial page

costs more than any other editorial product. For another, if it does its job right it is likely to be troublesome. A paper that lets sleeping dogs lie is not going to be disturbed by angry customers, whether from the lunatic fringe that doesn't like flouridation or from the quiet but authoritative voices of the power structure. Nor is a businessman board of directors going to raise eyebrows if all is kept obediently quiet. . . . No doubt it is this inherent dilemma that accounts for the diminishing editorial and the compensatory rise of the column. Pundits, trained seals, and I-was-there by-liners can be hired at a dime a dozen, and merchandized lavishly at little cost on the ed or op-ed page [the page positioned opposite the editorial page]. Speaking for themselves rather than the paper, such syndicated sages may be allowed to bellow as loudly as they like without risking more than an inch or two of skin off management's back. . . .

Editorial writing remains the soul of journalism, and journalism falls down on the job if it doesn't turn its prophets loose. Who ever heard of a gagged Isaiah, a mealy-mouthed Jeremiah? Yet many of today's editorial writers are not allowed the self-disciplined freedom that a confused and troubled country could use.[8]

So much for the influence of ownership, in all its various shadings. What other factors come into play as the opinion writer sets about his task of fashioning a policy stand?

BUT WHERE'S THE PARADE?

One consideration that is usually present somewhere in the opinion writer's consciousness is a concern not to get too far ahead of the reader. Most columnists and editorial writers operate on the assumption that the ideas they advance and the causes they push must not be ones that will seem too far-out in the eyes of the persons they are trying to influence.

If the editorialist comes out with proposals that will be perceived as unrealistically radical or premature, he may find himself playing drum major all by himself, with the rest of the parade several blocks back. As an editorial writer in a New England paper once observed:

> The greatest limitation on the free expression of candid opinion is not particularly the requirement of the publisher or editor, but the danger of getting too far out of line with contemporary prejudices. The toughest boss I have is the people who read the paper, damn 'em.[9]

This is an instinctive attitude on the part of opinion writers, sometimes backed up by experience. Campaigns for massive reforms have sometimes foundered, while bite-by-bite, gradual attacks on a problem have succeeded.

Some of the communication theorists offer support to the instinctive concern of the editorialists. Wilbur Schramm, one of the most distinguished writers in the field of communication theory and research, points out that when we try to communicate effectively with other people we need to be concerned that we do not conflict too directly with the way our audience sees and catalogs the world. A pilot, says Schramm, doesn't land crosswind unless he has to.[10]

But to some of the younger writers, particularly the militant journalists of advocacy, the concept of gradualism, staying within hailing distance of the reader's present position, is repugnant. They reject this approach as a cop-out and prefer an all-or-nothing pitch. And they, too, can find some encouragement in certain communication research findings.

One study, for example, produced the conclusion that the *more extreme* the degree of change the communicator attempts to bring about, the more *actual opinion change* he is likely to get in his target audience. It should be noted, however, that this was a controlled experiment study using students as subjects; it also utilized a high credibility source as communicator (someone whose ideas the students held in high regard). To what extent the study's findings would apply to the real-life situation of the opinion writer for the mass media can only be guessed.[11]

BOOSTING THE HOME TEAM

Another factor that the opinion writer weighs when determining what stand he will take on an issue is regionalism. A newspaper is published in and for a community, sometimes a large one, sometimes only a hamlet. Collectively or corporately the paper is a citizen of the community and is identified with the welfare of the community. So is the local broadcasting outlet. The writers for these local media tend to view developments in terms of how those developments will impinge on the community and its interests. Inevitably this becomes a significant factor in the shaping of editorial policy. Examples are easy to collect.

One East Coast paper had long been a supporter of the concept of freer international trade and a lowering of tariff barriers. Then one of the editorial writers for the paper undertook to explore, with a leading economist at a nearby university, what would result if tariffs were abandoned altogether by the United States, as a unilateral gesture toward improved international trade. He learned that much of American industry would be unaffected, since it depended so greatly on automated production. But he also found that in certain industries, where labor costs represented a major part of the overall expenses of production, the inroads that would be made by foreign products if tariffs were abandoned would be disastrous for the American producers. And the industries most likely to be affected were the very ones that were the backbone of the economy in the editorial writer's state. So he rushed back to his typewriter to modify the paper's policy on free trade, not to abandon the traditional stand but to amend it to provide for federal aid to relocate industries disproportionately injured by tariff reduction. Regionalism had to be served.

Another paper that had many times adopted liberal positions on minimum-wage laws suddenly backpedaled when a proposal was made to extend the wage floor provisions to farm labor. One of the local industries was the growing of crops that were picked by youngsters recruited for short-term summer jobs. The editorialist came out against the minimum-wage plan, gravely noting that "an old economists' axiom warns against precipitous changes affecting wealth-producing mainstays of our nation."

Kenneth Rystrom, editorial page editor of the *Columbian* of Vancouver, Washington, wrote in *Masthead,*

> We suffer from narrowness of horizon. Too many of us can't see beyond the limits of our circulation areas. We approve of developments (new industry, congressional appropriations, population growth) that seem to boost our community. We disapprove of developments that seem to hurt our community. What's good for General Motors (if we have a big General Motors plant in our area) is good for the country. . . . Our concern for our local interests gives us a distorted view of the world. . . .
>
> We view the issues of the day from our cramped bailiwicks and pronounce judgments. The world, as seen by the American press (including august editorial writers), consists of countless little dukedoms, few of them overlapping, even fewer in meaningful contact with each other. [12]

Two writers for the *Columbia Journalism Review* documented the influence of regionalism on editorial policy dramatically in a particular instance involving a large number of newspapers and their reaction to a

McCall's magazine article challenging local pride. *McCall's* had published in its November 1968 issue an article entitled "Drink At Your Own Risk." It described investigations into drinking-water quality that had been conducted by the U.S. Public Health Service and noted that the water supplies in 102 cities in 32 states and Puerto Rico had been placed on a "provisionally approved" list. This meant that the water provided to the populations of these cities was in some degree below standard, though not in every case seriously below standard.

The two writers for the *Review,* David M. Rubin and Stephen Landers, made a check to see how the newspapers in the 102 cities responded to the article's charge that their citizens were drinking water that might be of questionable quality. They found that most of the papers took a hostile and defensive position, seeking to discredit the charge and offer support to the local waterworks. Only a few papers launched full-scale investigations of their communities' situation to determine whether abuses and problems really did exist.[13]

HEAVIEST ON THE SCALE

There are of course a good many other factors that find a place on the scales when an opinion writer sets about his task of weighing and judging. Some are buried deep in the makeup, background, education, and intellectual conditioning of the writer—all that has gone into the building of the frame of reference through which he personally views the world. (John Oakes, editorial page editor of the *New York Times,* once acknowledged that he had changed his mind—and the paper's policy—about the vote for 18-year-olds because he had observed the "serious and genuine interest" that his two daughters and their friends appeared to have in what was going on.)[14]

But of all of the forces and influences that come to bear, consciously and unconsciously, when the opinion writer decides what stand to take, there is one that is omnipresent and all-pervasive for *most* editorialists on *most* communication media. That is an honest concern that the public interest be served.

There are no research findings to cite in support of the assertion in that last paragraph. It is advanced simply as an article of faith, based on a quarter century of personal experience as an opinion writer, as a close observer of the opinion function in all media, and as a teacher in the field of journalism. Most of the editorialists the author has known—and they are many—have had a genuine sense of dedication to trying to give the best effort they could to the job of analyzing and counseling their readers. Their motives often were mixed and included some of those discussed earlier in this chapter. But the concept of safeguarding and improving the public welfare was always a part of the philosophy by which they were guided—or so it has seemed to the author. The reader will have to develop his own conclusions.

NOTES

1. Jack Boynton, quoted in *Editor & Publisher,* March 8, 1969, p. 64.

2. This was the editorial conference of the *Providence Journal* and the *Evening Bulletin* of Providence, Rhode Island. The *Journal,* a morning paper, and the *Bulletin,* an afternoon paper, had at that time a single board of editorial writers and many, though not all, editorials ran in both papers. Each paper had its own editorial cartoonist.

3. Edwin L. Dale, Jr., "Behind the Myth of 'Editorial Policy,' " *Columbia Journalism Review,* Winter 1967–1968, p. 48.

4. John L. Hulteng, "Public Conceptions of Influences on Editorial Page Views," *Journalism Quarterly,* Summer 1969, pp. 362–364.

5. Cleveland Wilhoit and Dan Drew, "A Profile of the Editorial Writer," *Masthead,* Fall 1971, pp. 2–14.

6. "Presidential Endorsements: Consensus or Crisis?" a symposium, *Masthead,* Spring 1965.

7. Arthur Ochs Sulzberger, quoted in "How *New York Times* Shapes Its Opinions," by Cheng Tan, *Editor & Publisher,* August 22, 1970, pp. 18 and 22.

8. Herbert Brucker, "The Prophet Motive," *Masthead,* Summer 1970, pp. 9–12.

9. John Lofton, "Can Editorial Writers Afford to Deal with Their Publishers as Equals?" *Masthead,* Winter 1950–1951, p. 1.

10. In Wilbur Schramm, *The Process and Effects of Mass Communication,* Urbana, University of Illinois Press, 1965, p. 14.

11. The study is described in Marvin Karlins and Herbert I. Abelson, *Persuasion,* New York, Springer Publishing Co., 1970, pp. 126–127.

12. Kenneth Rystrom, "Provincialism as a Vested Interest," *Masthead,* Spring 1970, pp. 6–7.

13. David M. Rubin and Stephen Landers, "National Exposure and Local Coverup: A Case Study," *Columbia Journalism Review,* Summer 1969, pp. 17–22.

14. Cheng Tan, "How *New York Times* Shapes Its Opinions," *op. cit.,* p. 22.

5
What Target
in the Sights?

All communication is aimed at some audience. Even the lone cry of anguish in the wilderness presumably intends heaven as the auditor. And opinion writing by its nature very definitely is shaped for the attention of a specific set of readers or listeners. But what set, exactly?

If the vehicle we are considering is an opinion journal with a strong ideological flavor, the question of what target is in the sights pretty much answers itself. The writer for such a journal knows that he is writing largely to like-minded persons, a self-selected group already inclined to agree with the viewpoints he is advancing. His function is largely that of exhorting the faithful to new heights of dedication, providing them with fresh ammunition to use in converting the unbelievers, and unearthing for them new arguments that are congruent with the point of view they already hold. He interprets each new development in the news according to the party-line gospel, whether Right, Left, or counter-culture.

But the opinion writer for the publication of general circulation confronts a challenge considerably more complex. He knows that his publication, or his broadcast, goes out to a whole spectrum of readers, not to just one narrow segment. He knows that his audience includes some who are very well informed and some who know little or nothing about the topics he proposes to discuss, some who have an intense personal stake and others who are almost totally indifferent to the events of the day. How should he take aim at this vast, heterogeneous, faceless mass? What target should he envision as he squares up to the typewriter?

TWO SCHOOLS OF THOUGHT

From the earliest days of editorial writing there has been a division among opinion writers on this point. Some have insisted that they would speak to all of the potential audience; others have argued that persuasion ought to be aimed at the elite, who would then pass the word on to the tractable masses.

Joseph Pulitzer voiced the philosophy of the first school when he said that "I want to address a nation, not a select committee." Arthur Brisbane, who wrote first for Pulitzer and later for Hearst, was perhaps the most consistent exponent of this reach-for-everybody philosophy.

Brisbane was for a time on the staff of Pulitzer's *New York World,* but Hearst hired him to come over to the *New York Journal* in 1897, with the specific mission of building circulation through a hard-hitting editorial page. And that Brisbane did, helping to bring the *Journal's* readership up from 40,000 to 1,000,000 and becoming the highest-paid editor in the world in the process. (During the 1920s Brisbane reputedly earned $275,000 a year as editorial writer and syndicated columnist.) He developed a writing style as an editorialist that was simple, short, vigorous—specifically designed to appeal to the masses. He once observed: "It is not possible for the individual to invent a language, but he may make it more effective by loud talking."[1]

The Brisbane approach of trying for the widest possible readership is followed in some editorial sections today. The brisk, blunt, but effectively written editorial page of the *New York Daily News* is one of those.

The proponents of the second school of thought relied on a trickledown process. They reasoned that if you could frame a message that would reach and impress the leadership crust of society, the influentials, then these powerful few would affect the masses; there would be no need to make an effort to speak directly to the entire potential audience.

Edwin L. Godkin, who wrote for the *Nation* and the *New York Post* in the late nineteenth century, was usually cited as the most successful exponent of this approach. And his views were indeed reflected in other journals and newspapers around the country and quoted by preachers and lecturers, thus multiplying the impact of his thoughts.

Some of the present-day columnists and commentators are widely reprinted or quoted and presumably are also achieving the same sort of multiplier effect with their persuasive messages.

WILL THE REAL ELITE PLEASE STAND?

From the beginning, however, there were flaws in the reasoning that underlay the trickle-down approach. The assumption was made that the influentials who were going to pass on the message to the masses were the economic, political, and social leaders of the day. And it was further assumed that the way to impress these leaders was by means of an elaborate, ornate writing style, heavily studded with literary allusions and enriched with a polysyllabic vocabulary.

But communication researchers, as they began probing into the process of opinion formation, developed findings that suggested that these early assumptions were not well-founded. The ideas and opinions of the mass media are indeed absorbed first by a relatively small group of persons in the community and then passed on to a larger group—but not in the way that the trickle-down theorists posited.

Beginning with a classic study of three election campaigns of the 1930s and 1940s by Paul Lazarsfeld, Bernard Berelson, and Helen Gaudet, researchers confirmed that there does exist a set of influentials who have an impact on the opinion formation and attitude change of groups of others who are typically followers. These influentials pay attention to the mass media of communication and then hand on information and ideas they get from these media to their followers, who themselves may not attend directly to the media. The researchers at first termed this process a *two-step flow*. Later they developed additional insights that suggested there was a multi-step flow (or n-step flow) with widening successive circles of influentials and opinion followers.

On the surface, these findings would seem to offer support to the proponents of the trickle-down school of opinion writing. But the researchers' discoveries went one important step further: The influentials they identified were not the intellectual, social, or economic elite that had originally been assumed to be the opinion leaders. Instead, the influentials tended to be persons within the close circle of acquaintances of those being influenced—in the home, at the shop, or at the plant. Rarely were they social or business superiors; they shared the economic status of those over whom they exerted an influence. The trickle, it appeared, was not down, but on a plane.

Other researchers later undertook additional studies and filled in the picture of the influential in greater detail. They discovered, for example, that there is specialization in opinion leadership. Within a given circle, one influential may be looked to for counsel on what kinds of food or wine to buy, while a quite different person may serve as the guide in political matters.

It was also determined that while opinion leaders tend to be exposed far more to the mass media than are the followers who are influenced by them, the influentials typically are more skeptical of the messages they get from the media than are the opinion-follower types.[2]

What guidance do these research findings provide for the opinion writer who is trying to decide what his target ought to be out there beyond the typewriter or the TV camera?

It would seem clear that his persuasive messages, if they get through at all, will very likely pass through a multi-step flow, with groups of influentials as intermediaries. But those influentials may be anywhere and everywhere in the potential audience; they can't be singled out as the intellectual crust or the social elite. They are in all walks of life, at every stage on the ideological spectrum, at every age level. The one thing they have in common is their tendency to pay close attention to the content of the media.

So if any rule of thumb is to be drawn up, it may well be that Pulitzer's injunction to address the nation would serve as well as anything. The opinion writer for the mass media (not the specialized journal, where audience characteristics can be identified more precisely) ought to frame his arguments clearly and simply enough so that they can be understood by nearly anyone among his potential audience. He ought to avoid the ornate flourish, the esoteric term, or the cryptic allusion that might perhaps score a point with the intellectual specialist, but which might only turn off most of his audience.

This does not mean, however, emulating the supersimplified approach of a Brisbane. Clear and understandable writing does not have to be monosyllabic or shallow. Graceful style, sound reasoning, and clarity of expression are not incompatible; on the contrary, they are all essential characteristics of effective opinion writing.

HOW OFTEN IN THE BULL'S-EYE?

Once he has identified the target he would like to reach, what kind of impact can the opinion writer reasonably hope to have on that target? Is he only shooting arrows into the air, after all?

As was noted in Chapter 2, the present-day editorialist cannot expect to emulate Greeley and set a nation marching while he counts cadence.

But he can count on having some impact on a more modest scale. As one editorial page editor, Robert B. Frazier of the *Eugene* (Oreg.) *Register-Guard,* put it:

> It will be a sad day for America if the newspaper editorial page—or any other medium of opinion—becomes so influential that it can "deliver the vote." People are too smart to follow blindly like that. The editorial page, we hope, will continue to be a liberalizing influence, a forum, a marketplace of ideas, a catalyst, a goad to public opinion. That's all we want it to be. If we ever take a part in developing a core of readers who follow this page or any other page every time, on every issue, we shall have failed.[3]

Measuring the more modest impact of the modern opinion writer is a baffling and uncertain matter. There are so many variables involved in attitude change and opinion formation that the isolation of the effect of any one of them is virtually impossible. What measurements have been taken are approximate rather than precise.

For example, a California researcher, James E. Gregg, sought to determine how influential a group of 11 California newspapers had been in the elections held between 1948 and 1962. He studied election results to see how many of the candidates who had received newspaper endorsement had won; he also determined whether these successful candidates had run up larger victory margins in the circulation areas of the papers supporting them than they had in the state or district at large. On the basis of his findings, he concluded that the newspaper editorial endorsements indeed were influential and that they appeared to have been more influential in local elections than in state or national races. But his conclusions had to be tempered, since they in effect attributed a result to a single variable in situations where many variables were involved. The findings clearly suggested the *possibility* that the editorial endorsements had been effective, but it could not be said that the case had been proved.[4]

In 1970 Gregg replicated his first study, but this time he sought to measure the influence of the newspapers' endorsements on the fate of ballot measures rather than of candidates. He investigated the outcome of 195 elections involving 2,078 ballot propositions put before the voters during the period between 1948 and 1968.

As in the earlier study, he compared the percentage of "right" votes (those in support of the position taken by the paper) cast in the news-paper's home county with the percentage of right votes cast in the state as a whole and credited the difference in percentage points to the influence of the paper, but without claiming an exact statistical correla-tion.

In about one-third of the cases he found a negative correlation be-tween the papers' endorsement and the apparent effect on the voting outcome; in other words, the fact of the papers' support had apparently worked to the disadvantage of the ballot measure involved. The author concluded, as he had in the first study, that the newspapers' influence had been greatest when the voters had little or no other information on which to base a judgment.[5]

Another study, carried out on a different basis, produced somewhat different results. This involved an attempt to measure what impact the editorial endorsement of the *Toledo Blade* had on the fortunes of can-didates and issues in both local and statewide election races. In this study, the researchers questioned voters directly about the degree to which their ballot decision had been influenced by the *Blade's* endorse-ments. They concluded that the number of persons who, because of the newspaper's endorsement, had made a conscious decision at the ballot box ranged from 4 percent to 12 percent of the voters in the case of a statewide race (for governor) and from 2 percent to 4 percent in the case of a minor race (for state senate).[6] It is noteworthy that this finding is the reverse of that produced by Gregg, who concluded that newspaper endorsement had greater significance in local elections than in more general ones.

The percentage figures in the Toledo survey do not at first glance suggest that the paper had a very impressive impact on the voters. But, as the researchers noted, when the percentages are translated into votes cast, they mean that the endorsement of the *Blade* was worth from 5,500 to 15,600 votes in the gubernatorial contest and from 1,500 to 3,000 votes in the state senate race. And they concluded: "The power of the press in Toledo is real and important. This fact is particularly true since the politics of the area is competitive and many elections are decided by narrow margins."

Once again, it is necessary to caution that such isolated studies as these cannot be taken as generally representative. Most scholarly ver-dicts on the influence of the media of communication on public opin-ion tend to be phrased in broad terms rather than precise percentages, and for good reason.

POWER, EVEN IF UNSEEN

Still, the scholars do advance views that seem to indicate that the opinion function of the media is a pervasive, if difficult-to-measure force. The following is from Joseph T. Klapper:

> The media of mass communication may well exercise extensive social effects upon the masses by the indirect road of affecting the elite. Particular vehicles of mass communication (e.g., *The New York Times*) and other vehicles directed toward a more specialized audience (e.g., *The Wall Street Journal,* or *U.S. News and World Report*) may reasonably be supposed to affect the decisions and behavior of policy-making elites. Individual business and political leaders may or may not be "opinion leaders" in the sense in which the term is used in communication research—i.e., they may or may not critically influence a handful of their peers. But their decisions and their consequent behavior in themselves affect society at large, and the mere fact of their taking a particular stand frequently serves to make that stand and the issue to which it pertains a topic of media reporting and debate, and a topic in regard to which personal influence, in the more restricted sense of the term, is exercised. The media may, in short, stimulate the elite to actions which affect the masses and which incidentally restimulate and so affect both the media and the channels of interpersonal influence.[7]

Two other communication researchers, Kurt and Gladys Lang, have identified several ways in which the media of mass communication exert power over opinion change and attitude formation in society.[8] The Langs suggest that the media affect public attitudes by *disseminating distrust* of political figures and political processes by emphasizing the disorder and malfunctioning of those processes rather than their efficiency, their failures rather than their accomplishments ("bad" news is bigger news than "good" news). This sort of effect was clearly evident during the last year of Lyndon Johnson's presidency; negative comment appeared almost daily in the work of satirical columnists such as Art Buchwald. An official of the next administration to come to power apparently felt that the process was continuing. Daniel Moynihan, White House advisor to President Richard Nixon, contended that the press was undermining the presidency and making it difficult, if not impossible, to run an effective federal government.

On the other hand, according to the Langs, the media also may affect public opinion by channeling trust, that is, by providing a dignified platform or impressive sponsorship for the pronouncements and activities of officials. At times the media seem almost to be mounting a myth-building campaign around certain favored figures; both Dwight Eisenhower and John Kennedy were beneficiaries of such treatment.

It would be impossible to set a yardstick against media activities of either negative or positive thrust to measure precisely their impact. But we can nevertheless sense with some certainty that they *do* have impact.

Still another communication scholar, Bernard Berelson, points out a further way in which the opinion function of the communication media can play a role in public opinion formation and change:

> The media are effective in structuring political issues for their audiences. For example, there is a tendency for partisans on each side of a controversial matter to agree with their own side's arguments in the order in which those arguments are emphasized in mass communications. Thus, the media set the political stage, so to speak, for the ensuing debate. In addition, there is some evidence that private discussions of political matters take their cue from the media's presentation of issues; people talk politics along the lines laid down in the media.[9]

As a final witness to the power of the media of mass communication to influence the nation's thinking and actions, let's bring to the witness box not another scholar, but author Theodore H. White:

> All politicians operate in an environment of ideas. But, technically, this environment changes from decade to decade. Whoever shapes the ideas, whoever creates the applause or the denunciation, or whoever seizes the moral heights in the world of ideas controls the politics not of today but of ten years hence. The common phrase in New York is that the New York *Times* can't carry an election. The New York *Times* editorial page can't swing even 100,000 votes in any given contemporary New York City election. But it affects the thinking of all executive, intellectual, and communications leadership. And ten years hence this thinking *does* shape elections; it creates the sounding board against which our politicians offer programs and leadership.[10]

These various assessments seem to support the conclusion (even in the absence of authoritative tables of statistics) that the opinion function of the media of mass communication does have an influence on the shaping of public attitudes and actions. It is a leverage worth wielding.

NOTES

1. An excellent profile of Brisbane, from which some of the above is taken, is "The Paradox That Was Arthur Brisbane," by Ray Vanderburg, *Journalism Quarterly*, Summer 1970, pp. 281–286.

2. The original study was reported in Paul Lazarsfeld, Bernard Berelson, and Helen Gaudet, *The People's Choice*, New York, Duell, Sloan & Pierce, 1944. An article that reviews later research in the area is "The Two-Step Flow Theory: Cross-Cultural Implications," by Lloyd R. Bostian, *Journalism Quarterly*, Spring 1970, pp. 109–117. See also *Media and Non-Media Effects on the Formation of Public Opinion*, American Institute for Political Communication, Washington, D.C., 1969.

3. Robert B. Frazier, in an editorial, "How Much Influence Do We Have?" published in the *Eugene* (Oreg.) *Register-Guard*, Oct. 9, 1957.

4. James E. Gregg, "Newspaper Editorial Endorsements and California Elections, 1948–62," *Journalism Quarterly*, Autumn 1965, pp. 532–538.

5. This study by James E. Gregg is summarized in *ANPA News Research Bulletin No. 17*, December 2, 1971, published by the American Newspaper Publishers Association News Research Foundation.

6. Norman Blume and Schley Lyons, "The Monopoly Newspaper in a Local Election: The Toledo *Blade*," *Journalism Quarterly*, Summer 1968, pp. 286–292.

7. Joseph T. Klapper, "The Effects of Mass Communication," in *Reader in Public Opinion and Communication*, edited by Bernard Berelson and Morris Janowitz, New York, Free Press, pp. 473–486.

8. Kurt Lang and Gladys E. Lang, "The Mass Media and Voting," in Berelson and Janowitz, *ibid.*, pp. 455–472.

9. Bernard Berelson, "Communication and Public Opinion," in *The Process and Effects of Mass Communication*, edited by Wilbur Schramm, Urbana, University of Illinois Press, 1965, pp. 342–356.

10. Theodore H. White, "America's Two Cultures," *Columbia Journalism Review*, Winter 1969–1970, p. 9.

6
Developing Editorial Ideas

An old southern recipe for rabbit stew begins: "First, you get your rabbit." So far as concocting an editorial is concerned, the rabbit, the essential first step, is an idea—a well-reasoned, arresting, pertinent idea— and it often proves to be as elusive and as hard to catch up with as the stew ingredient.

It is fair to say that editorial writers are valued more for their ability to come up with ideas than for their skill at clothing those ideas in persuasive language, although that is obviously also important. The opinion writer spends much of his working day reading, thinking, sorting out possibilities, testing alternatives; the actual writing of editorials may occupy only a small part of his time.

Editorials without ideas are empty shells of rhetoric that are a waste of newspaper space or broadcast time (though, unhappily, a good many of that variety find their way into print or onto the air).

To be worth newsprint or air time, an editorial must have something to offer to the reader or listener. It must *explain something, identify issues* involved in a controversy, *advance an interpretation* of a news event, *make a case* either for or against a cause or an action—or maybe do all of these at the same time.

This is why Chapter 2 laid so heavy an emphasis on the necessity for the opinion writer to bring to his job a solid background of education and experience. Ideas bubble up out of a depth of understanding; they can't be conjured out of thin air.

So it is worth noting again: Anyone who wants to wield the opinion function ought to make himself an educated person, ought to plan on continuing the educational experience indefinitely, and ought to be fully able to draw efficiently and knowledgeably on a wide range of resources and references. (Some suggestions about references and research shortcuts that editorial writers have found particularly useful are cataloged later in this chapter.)

Assuming that he is thus well backgrounded, how does the opinion writer go about the specific assignment of formulating ideas? There he sits at his desk, a half dozen morning papers before him, specialized journals at his elbow, the policy framework of his publication surrounding him like a nimbus, a reminder of the overall directions he must keep in mind. Then what happens? How does he pick out of the welter of news and information in front of him and in his mind a fresh idea around which to build an editorial that will be a useful contribution to his audience?

A HELPFUL CHECKLIST

The writing of analysis is to a large extent a creative act. And creativity cannot easily be reduced to a pat formula. But there is an old and simple approach to anatomizing a problem and seeking its solution that the opinion writer can use with profit. It derives from philosopher John Dewey's description of how we think, and its application to editorial writing was made by Chilton R. Bush in his comprehensive *Editorial Thinking and Writing,* published 40 years ago.[1] There are four steps in the process:

1. The first step is to *identify the problem.* What is it, exactly, that you want to discuss or resolve? Is there something there that needs explanation or interpretation?

    This seems an absurdly simple point, at first blush. But a great many opinion writers never bother to take this first step. They sit down at their typewriters, a headline of the morning in mind, and begin pontificating—without ever asking the vital question: Is there really something that needs to be said on this topic? You can detect that sort of editorial at a glance; it wanders aimlessly, babbling like the conversationalist at a party who has launched off on a pointless tack and desperately struggles on, not knowing how to extricate himself.

    The fact is that there may not be a genuine editorial topic in much of the morning's news. Just because a story occupied two columns and was topped by a screaming banner headline doesn't mean that it must become an editorial page item. If an editorial does no more than repackage the news that has appeared elsewhere in the paper or magazine, it makes no useful contribution to the reader.

So make sure there is a problem—a complicated, mixed-up mess that needs to unraveled to be made meaningful; an issue on which a case needs to be made, in support or opposition; a half-truth in the news that needs to be revealed in full.

2. The next step in the Dewey-Bush formula is the *mustering of alternatives.* Once satisfied that there is a problem to be tackled, the editorial writer searches through his experience, his knowledge of the field he is considering, and the reference resources available to him, with the objective of dredging up as many possible solutions as he can identify. When several persons are involved, as in the editorial conference, this would involve *brainstorming* the question—putting out on the table every conceivable possibility, however farfetched or improbable it might appear at first view.

The point here is to avoid locking in on the first notion that comes to mind, the most obvious answer. Not until you have honestly appraised all of the possibilities—or at least all that you and your colleagues can think of—can you claim to have analyzed the issue. Sometimes the process of canvassing the possibilities is itself a spur to creativity, and a hitherto unexplored avenue may open up.

3. Now begin *testing the altervatives,* one by one. Set each one up and check it out critically to see whether it would be likely to stand the tests of reality. Some can be discarded quickly as being too full of flaws and bugs to be practicable. Others will hold up better under scrutiny and make it to the semifinals.

4. By process of testing and elimination, work your way down to the *most likely answer* or the *most useful solution* to the question or problem, and then organize it for presentation to your reader or listener.

This is perhaps as compact and useful an approach for the opinion writer to use in identifying and developing an editorial idea as any that could be suggested. It may not apply to every situation, to be sure, and the writer may not always proceed step by step through the full sequence. But if you want a checklist to run through, as a pilot does to make sure his ship is ready to take off, this well tested one will do.

BACKSTOPS IN THE LIBRARY—AND ELSEWHERE

As was noted earlier in this chapter, the opinion writer should be able to draw on a variety of reference resources. At each stage of the four-step process that was outlined, he is likely to need to turn to a current newspaper or two, a magazine or journal report of a month ago, a volume from the editorial library, or the thoughts of a colleague—either on the editorial staff or from the news department.

An opinion writer who attempts to rely only on what he can keep stored in his head will not contribute much as a generator of ideas.

If he is a specialist, the opinion writer will of course keep himself well posted on his own field, through books as well as periodicals. But he must also be a generalist, and his reading is likely to be catholic in its range.

Robert B. Frazier, writing in *Masthead,* reported on a survey he had made of the regular reading diet of 59 of his colleagues in the membership of the National Conference of Editorial Writers:

> A large share of the editorial writer's reading, especially on the smaller newspapers, is done in periodicals. Many subscribed to a great number of newspapers. Thirty-eight say they see the *New York Times.* This is followed by the *Wall Street Journal* with 24, the *[Christian Science] Monitor* with 21 and the *Washington Post* with 18. Regionally, there are differences. Midwesterners are likely to see the *Post-Dispatch,* the Chicago papers or the *Kansas City Star.* Southerners favor the *Atlanta Constitution.* Westerners like the *San Francisco Chronicle.* Several mentioned the *Los Angeles Times,* but only one was a westerner.[2]

He listed the magazines favored by the 59 respondents to his survey, with the number of editorial writers who in each case claimed that they read the magazine regularly:

New York Times (Sunday edition), 37; *Harper's,* 32; *Time,* 29; *Newsweek,* 24; *National Observer,* 23; *Life,* 23; *Reporter,* 23; *Atlantic,* 22; *U.S. News and World Report,* 18; *New Yorker,* 17; *National Review,* 17; *Insider's News Letter,* 17; *Saturday Evening Post,* 16; *Reader's Digest,* 14; *Look,* 14; *Business Week,* 12; *New Republic,* 10; *Human Events,* 6; *Progressive,* 6; *Christian Century,* 6; *Commonweal,* 6; *Nation,* 4; *Changing Times,* 4; *Farm Journal,* 4; *Scientific American,* 3; *I. F. Stone's Weekly,* 3; *America,* 3; *Fortune,* 1.

What is perhaps most arresting about that list (and most disheartening, too) is the fact that the so-called opinion journals—such as *National Review* on the Right and the *Nation, New Republic,* or *Progressive on* the Left—are read regularly by so far fewer of the editorialists than are some of the more general, entertainment-oriented periodicals such as *Life, Look,* or *Reader's Digest.* Frazier's findings in this respect were similar to those of the author when, two years earlier, he had surveyed 38 Oregon editors:

The magazines which appeared most often on the 38 editors' lists were *Life* with 20 mentions, and *Time* with 19. *Saturday Evening Post* and *Reader's Digest* came next with 18 mentions apiece. Then came *U.S. News* with 17 and *Newsweek* with 14. . . . It was interesting . . . to note that four publications which represent extremes of opinion on the Left and Right—*Nation, New Republic, Human Events,* and *National Review*—were not included in the "regularly read" list by a single one of the responding editors.[3]

Frazier's *Masthead* survey indicated that the editorial writers keep up with trade publications or professional journals that specialize in shoptalk and improvement of the breed. These include *Masthead,* the quarterly publication of the National Conference of Editorial Writers; *Editor & Publisher,* a weekly trade magazine; *Quill,* a monthly publication of Sigma Delta Chi, Professional Journalistic Society; *Nieman Reports,* a quarterly of press criticism published by the Nieman Foundation of Harvard University; *Columbia Journalism Review,* a bimonthly published by Columbia University and perhaps the best of the journals of press criticism; *Journalism Quarterly,* the scholarly publication aimed at journalism educators; and a few others.

AT THE EDITORIAL ELBOW

In addition to the flow of daily, weekly, and monthly periodicals, the opinion writer relies heavily on standard works of reference of various kinds. In his book, *Facts in Perspective,* Hillier Krieghbaum reported on a survey taken of 25 editorial writers attending a seminar of the American Press Institute. They were asked to list their favorite general references and came up with the following:

> *World Almanac*—19; *Who's Who in America, Congressional Record, Quarterly* and *Directory* (the three as a group); and *Editorial Research Reports*—13 each; *Encyclopedia Britannica*—10; *The Encyclopedia Americana; Facts on File;* and *World Report*—7 each; Webster's dictionary—6; *Statesman's Yearbook* and Bartlett's *Familiar Quotations*—5 each; *Bible and Concordance*—4; *Annals of the American Academy of Political and Social Science,* and *Information Please Almanac*—3 each.[4]

A more exhaustive compilation of useful reference works was put together by a single editorial page editor, the same Robert B. Frazier whose survey of editors' magazine-reading habits was quoted earlier. In the Summer 1963 issue of *Masthead,* Frazier published an article titled "The Editorial Elbow—Being a more-or-less compleat listing of reference works useful, day by day, to the editor, reporter, and copyreader."

In the article he not only lists but informatively annotates a comprehensive collection of basic tools such as dictionaries and atlases and supplementary sources such as anthologies, directories, and special services of value to the opinion writer. Anyone who would like to get a sense of the range of backstop resources an editorial writer ought to know about and have on tap should read through the Frazier piece. It appears on pages 5 through 16 of the *Masthead* issue, Vol. 15, No. 3.

Two of the citations that appear on both the list in Krieghbaum's book and the one in Frazier's article deserve somewhat fuller mention here. They are *Congressional Quarterly* and *Editorial Research Reports,* both published by Congressional Quarterly Inc., in Washington, D.C.

Congressional Quarterly (*CQ*) comes out weekly rather than on the quarterly basis that its title suggests. It constitutes a condensed but thorough review of what has gone on in Washington the previous week —votes in both houses of Congress and their various committees; important actions in the various executive departments; court decisions of significance.

This weekly service, together with more elaborate *CQ* summaries published from time to time as monographs or paperbound books, represents an indispensable source of information for the editorial writer whose publication does not have its own Washington bureau.[5]

The other half of the combination, *Editorial Research Reports* (*ERR*), in effect amounts to a syndicated reference service for opinion writers. It sends out a daily mailing with brief but useful references to topics that are in the news—or will soon be coming up in the news. Each week a much longer *ERR* pamphlet appears (5,000 to 6,000 words), usually devoted to a single current issue and rounding up background facts, statistics, quotations and source references—the very raw material the editorialist needs.

OUT OF THE CAN

Some of the weekly *ERR* pamphlets are so comprehensive that they could serve as editorials of explanation just as they are. And in fact some newspaper and magazine opinion sections make generous use of quotes and excerpts from *ERR* publications—sometimes even passing them off as their own, without attribution to the original publisher.

The editorial page editor jealous of his reputation would not indulge in such deception of his readers; but there are a few who aren't so particular. To such opinion writers of flexible morality there are some even more flagrant shortcuts available.

Under the title "Editorial Writing Made Easy," Louis M. Lyons, then curator of the Nieman Foundation at Harvard, described in 1948 the operation of a "canned editorial" factory.[6]

This organization, E. Hofer and Sons of Portland, Oregon, sent out prefabricated editorials on behalf of power interests, particularly those in opposition to federal power projects. Lyons found that 59 newspapers, with a total circulation of 390,000, had used these editorials as their own, without any indication to the reader that they had been written elsewhere by a special-interest group with an ax to grind. As Lyons put it: "This outfit has discovered that there are editors either too lazy to write their own editorials, or venal enough to present the paid-for propaganda of special interests as their own views."

Apparently the angry criticism of the Harvard curator did not discourage the canned editorial factory (even if it perhaps shamed some editors into mending their ways). Nearly a quarter century later the following appeared in *Masthead,* written by the director of the Tennessee Valley Authority:[7]

> My complaint is with the newspapers of the country who prostitute their editorial responsibility by publishing as their own editorials the products of anonymous propaganda boiler plate sweatshops. It is disheartening to report that there are still many such papers over the nation, and they are not all country weeklies or suburban shopper throwaways.
>
> I find that many papers in all parts of the country are still great users and consumers of "canned" editorials which come along with the other junk mail from public relations firms like E. Hofer and Sons of Hillsboro, Oregon. Through their *Industrial News Review,* Hofer and Sons have for half a century attempted to spare the newspapers of the country the burden of writing editorials, by preparing them all in advance and free of charge.

There are, of course, not just one but many firms engaged in turning out prefabricated opinion pieces for the use of lazy, complaisant, or overworked editors. Happily, most of their output goes into the wastebasket rather than into the editorial pages—but not all, by any means.

The opinion writer who respects himself and his important function searches widely for information and insights. But he does his own thinking. And he tries to serve the public interest, not that of some hidden persuader.

A WORKING GROUP

One significant reason why a great many editorial writers do respect their craft, and approach it seriously and conscientiously, is the nature of the principal professional society in their field—the National Conference of Editorial Writers (NCEW). Unlike some counterpart associations elsewhere in journalism, NCEW is a working organization. Its annual meetings center on critique sessions in which members painstakingly and unsparingly point out the warts and blemishes in the editorial page products of their fellows and then submit to some of the same treatment in turn.

Looking back over the first two decades of NCEW meetings, one of the founders of the organization, Dwight Sargent, once editor of the editorial page of the *New York Herald Tribune* and later curator of the Nieman Foundation at Harvard University, observed:

> Every convention of every professional or business group has as its goal, to some degree, the edification of its membership. No similar organization, however, allots as much time to the critical examination of its own work as the NCEW. This is the best witness to its sense of responsibility to the nation's newspaper readers, and to the nation's newspaper publishers. The critiques have been singularly successful, not only in making editorial pages more attractive typographically, but in expanding their role as a source of influence in our society.[8]

The quarterly publication of NCEW is *Masthead*, an unpretentious, simply printed journal filled with earnest shoptalk and penetrating observations on the state of the art. It circulates to the 300 to 400 members of NCEW and to a scattering of journalism educators and university libraries; in absolute numbers it has a miniscule following. But its influence ripples out through the field and has a disproportionately significant effect on the standards of opinion writing throughout the nation. Each issue of *Masthead* reprints the NCEW's "Basic Statement of Principles" and also makes an effort to implement that statement, the preamble of which states:

> Journalism in general, editorial writing in particular, is more than another way of making money. It is a profession devoted to

the public welfare and to public service. The chief duty of its practitioners is to provide for the information and guidance toward sound judgment which are essential to the sound functioning of a democracy.

Of the numerous aids and references cited in this chapter, *Masthead* is probably the one more often found near the editor's elbow than any other, and with good reason.

NOTES

1. Chilton R. Bush, *Editorial Thinking and Writing,* New York, Appleton, 1932, pp. 72–85.

2. Robert B. Frazier, "What Do You Read, My Lord?" *Masthead,* Summer 1962, pp. 10–16.

3. John L. Hulteng, "Any Ideas in the Paper?" *Nieman Reports,* April 1960, pp. 13–15.

4. Hillier Krieghbaum, *Facts in Perspective,* Englewood Cliffs, N.J., Prentice-Hall, 1956, pp. 119–120.

5. In 1968 the *Congressional Quarterly* weekly report was going to 4,400 clients, including 400 of the nation's daily newspapers. The cost for the combined package of *CQ* and *Editorial Research Reports* ranged in 1968 from $8 a week for papers with less than 5,000 circulation to $85.50 a week for papers in the largest circulation category. The three big broadcasting networks paid $400 a week each. (From "Capital Watchers: Publishing Firm Makes Mark by Spotlighting Government, Politics," by Donald Moffit, in *Wall Street Journal,* September 25, 1968, pp. 1 and 18.

6. Louis M. Lyons, "Editorial Writing Made Easy," in *Reporting the News,* New York, Atheneum, 1968, pp. 81–91. This piece originally appeared as an article in the July 1948 issue of *Nieman Reports.*

7. Frank E. Smith, "Still too Many 'Canned' Editorials," *Masthead,* Summer 1971, pp. 26–28.

8. Dwight E. Sargent, "Twenty Years before the Masthead," *Nieman Reports,* December 1966, p. 12.

7
Constructing an Argument

If one were to lay out an opinion article on a dissection table, like a frog in a biology lab, it would be seen to have certain standard parts: a lead (or opening), a body, and a closing passage. This would be true of virtually any kind of opinion piece, whether a newspaper editorial, a magazine essay, or a broadcast commentary. (There are, to be sure, some variant approaches using a poetic or pictorial structure that would not conform exactly to the pattern, but the majority of opinion pieces have the standard parts, in conventional order.)

It might seem logical, then, to launch a discussion of the how-to-do-it of opinion writing by considering first the lead, or opening segment. That might seem logical, but it really isn't. So we won't begin that way.

As a practical matter, the opinion writer must concern himself first with the body of the article he is going to write. This does not mean that he plunks himself down at his typewriter and begins writing in the middle of the piece. But it does mean that until he has worked out the central theme, the basic line of argumentation he wants to unfold, the opinion writer cannot know what sort of opening gambit he might want to use. So the writer typically begins to build an editorial article by shaping the argument he proposes to advance. He may actually write it all out, or outline it in skeletal terms, or only mull it over and over in his mind while he stares vacantly at the asphalt roof or the office window across the street. But, one way or another, it is with the fashioning of his argument that he concerns himself first and longest. So it will be also with this text. We'll focus first on argumentation and case making, the heart of any opinion piece. In a later chapter we'll turn to consideration of openings, closings, and opinion writing style. This sequence may disconcert those readers of a tidy turn of mind who prefer to move along in orderly progression. But if they are willing to suspend judgment for a bit, they will eventually find all the pieces fitting together.

NOT *ALWAYS* FOR OR AGAINST

The emphasis placed on argumentation in the foregoing paragraphs should not be taken to mean that *every* opinion piece consists *wholly* of that ingredient. It is true that any opinion writing involves case making or argumentation to at least some degree. But the degree varies. Before looking at the various techniques of case making, it might be well to acknowledge in passing that there are some kinds of editorials, interpretive news articles, or magazine essays that are *primarily* definitional or explanatory in character. And these expository pieces have their part to play in the opinion function. The author, when still an editorial writer, looked at the matter thus:

> The expository editorial seeks to probe behind the facts of news, and sometimes ahead of them. Its success rests upon the experience and skill of the editorial writer. Ideally it should develop the news from two- to three-dimensional depth. At its worst, of course, the expository editorial becomes merely a clip-and-paste filler for a dull day or a lazy typewriter.
>
> But when properly used the expository piece gives a strength and reader value to the editorial page that could not be achieved in any editorial room guided by a rigid rule that every piece must "take a stand." There are many subjects in any day's news budget that do not lend themselves to pro–con editorial comment, but which could be treated to the reader's clear profit in an expository editorial.[1]

The expository or explanatory background piece or editorial may seek to help the reader by simply identifying the individuals or the backstage forces that may be contesting with one another in a given news development ("You can't tell the players without a scorecard!"). Often a heated exchange at the city council meeting in an argument over zoning, for example, will appear to be a dispute between, say, the mayor and the chairman of the zoning commission. But actually, behind the protagonists who are doing all the shouting, may be on the one hand a group of property owners hoping to make a killing and on the other hand a group of planners concerned about the long-range development of the community. The surface facts may be in the news. The *reality* may be brought out only in an editorial or an interpretive analysis.

Or the expository editorial or article may be designed to *explain something complex* so that the reader's understanding is broadened. One science writer devoted a whole series of pieces to what amounted to a short course in the functioning of hormones in the human body. He spent six months interviewing doctors and researchers, gathering information, schooling himself to do an educational, interpretive job for the reader. In his series he drew heavily on analogy, comparing the workings of the hormonal system with, say, the functioning of a car, something that is familiar to nearly all potential readers. ("The thyroid works like the accelerator, speeding up or slowing down bodily processes.")

Yet even in background articles where definition or explanation may be the chief purpose, some case making and argumentation is likely to come into the picture. And in most opinion writing, the *chief thrust* is that of argumentation—the unfolding of a sequence of evidence and a chain of reasoning designed to persuade the reader or auditor to adopt a point of view.

WHICH PART OF THE ICEBERG?

If persuasion is the principal objective of the opinion writer, he has some choices to make at the outset.

It has been suggested that man's decision-making process can be compared to an iceberg; the small part above water represents the rational, logical aspect of our approach to the development of an attitude or a conclusion; the vast, unseen bulk of the iceberg represents the powerful role that factors in our subconscious play in the making of decisions and the development of opinions.

Should the would-be persuader make use of the kinds of approaches that would affect the logical aspect of his audience's decision-making apparatus—the mustering of convincing evidence, the laying out of sound reasoning? Or should he utilize the visceral appeals (fear, self-interest) that trigger the hidden forces of the subconscious? Or is there some surefire combination of both approaches that can be plotted out?

Some modern observers of politics have suggested that the visceral approach is increasingly the most effective one in that field, where persuasion is altogether the name of the game.

Theodore H. White, in his "Making of the President" books, points out that political campaigns are more and more being conducted on an emotional basis. Issues all but vanish from the scene, while image and personality become paramount. The 1960 TV debates between Nixon and Kennedy, in which image seemed to play so significant a part, are often cited as an instance of this trend. And Joseph McGinnis, in *The Selling of the President, 1968,*[2] portrayed a campaign avowedly pegged to emotional, visceral appeals rather than to logic or reason.

But there is other evidence that also must be considered by the opinion writer. Research investigation of attitude formation and attitude change has explored both schools: the one holding that man is irrational, having limited powers of reason and reflection and being easily moved by emotional forces; and the other resting on the belief that man is basically a rational being, and that if he has enough evidence to work with, he will reason out a position on a logical basis.

Some of the findings of research suggest that each of us sometimes will act as a rational being, sometimes as an emotional one. To be sure, some personalities tend to be fixed strongly in one direction or the other; but most of us tend to react emotionally in one kind of situation and logically in another.

For example, in situations when prompt responses are called for, when we have little or no chance to look at alternatives, and when our own deep emotional needs are in some fashion aroused, we can be swayed by the devices of the propagandist. (In a mob situation, even the normally sober, serious-minded individual can be caught up in irrational frenzy.)

But in the kind of situation when there is more opportunity to examine possibilities and alternatives, and particularly when there are choices more complex than simple yes-or-no ones to be made, we tend to respond as rational beings, weighing argument and logic and rejecting simplistic fear or "gut" appeals.[3]

It would seem to be a reasonable assumption that the opinion writer for the media of mass communication is more often reaching his audience in the latter kind of situation—one in which there are complex choices and there is time to sort through alternatives. This isn't always the case, of course; on TV the circumstances in which visceral appeals can take effect may more often be present. But as a general rule, the opinion writer is not operating in a mob scene; he has good reason, then, to shun the propagandistic approaches and rely instead on logic, evidence, and argumentation. For the moment, let's continue this discussion on that assumption; later on there will be a chance to look at some kinds of situations in which the editorialist might with justification utilize simplistic, emotional appeals.

WAYS OF ARGUING

A persuasive case can be built in a variety of ways, whether it is intended for presentation in the course of a face-to-face argument or in the form of an analytical essay in some medium of mass communication.

Sometimes one person will try to convince another simply by the *force of authority*. This can be blunt and brutal, as when a dictatorial regime imposes a doctrine on a public. Or it can be much more defensible (though perhaps almost as direct), as when a columnist asserts an explanation or interpretation and expects his readers to believe it on the strength of his reputation alone.

Shortly after the announcement in the summer of 1971 that President Nixon would visit the People's Republic of China, a widely respected syndicated columnist, Roscoe Drummond, wrote:

> What does China most want now?
> I believe this is the answer:
>
> 1. Mao Tse-tung and Chou En-lai most want to avert a preemptive strike by the Soviet Union against its growing nuclear arsenal lest China's nuclear facilities be destroyed before they are sufficient to deter such a strike.
> 2. They want to persuade the Japanese not to go nuclear and to that end they aim to create an atmosphere of sufficient good will and confidence toward Japan so that it will not feel endangered. Closer U.S.—Chinese relations would help.
> 3. Now that the chaos of the Cultural Revolution is past, Red China wants to come out of its self-imposed isolation, become a force in world affairs, and more effectively compete with Moscow for leadership in the Communist world.
>
> It seems clear that Peking is convinced that more normal and more cordial relations with the United States will further all three of these objectives.[4]

There may be a few threads of evidence and argumentation built into those paragraphs here and there. But chiefly they constitute an assertion by Mr. Drummond about situations (what goes on in Mao's mind) that he cannot possibly know as facts. He offers them to the reader unsupported by evidence or argument, expecting that those who read his column will have developed enough confidence in his powers of analysis of foreign affairs to accept his version on faith. His expectation may well be justified, at least so far as a good many of his regular readers are concerned.

But most opinion writers do not have Roscoe Drummond's standing with their readers or listeners. They cannot simply say "we like this" or "we don't like that" and expect that this alone will persuade anyone. The typical editorialist cannot put much reliance on the argument from authority. As one such writer put it:

> He who would reach the minds, perhaps even the hearts, of others would do well not to pose as either a Moses or a Mencken, except, of course, if he had the genuine genius of either of those two. The mass of Americans now is too aware, too well educated, or too well turned off to words apart from deeds to respond to a slogan, a Chamber of Commerce propaganda piece, or a lament that things are not what they once were.[5]

WHAT BESIDES AUTHORITY?

So the vast majority of opinion writers who are neither Moses nor Mencken—nor even Drummond—must turn to other ways of arguing their views if they want to make any impression on their audience. Sometimes they build a case chiefly from *evidence*, hoping to pile up enough facts and interpretations of those facts so that the reader will be led to a conclusion.

If the issue to be resolved is whether the governor ought to be re-elected, the summing up of his record in factual terms may lead irresistibly to one verdict or the other.

Or if an editorialist without Mr. Drummond's established following had nevertheless wanted to argue that the Communist Chinese leaders had extended the invitation to Nixon primarily out of concern that Russia might attack their budding nuclear facilities, he might have arrayed a series of items of evidence pointing toward this conclusion: border clashes of increasing intensity, intelligence reports of Russian overflights of the Chinese nuclear complex in the Asian desert, the timetable of atomic-weapon testing carried out by the Chinese and monitored by Western radar and seismographic stations.

The effectiveness of a case built largely on evidence will depend on several factors. First, if the evidence is factual in nature, are the facts well-accepted and verifiable? Or are they "facts" only because the editorialist tries to fix that label on them?

Second, if the evidence is in the form of opinion, does that opinion come from an authority the reader will probably accept? Citing the opinion of a rock music star as to the prospects for the betterment of relations between Russia and the United States hardly constitutes reference to a valid source. To be sure, Americans have a long-standing habit of investing celebrity—however attained and in whatever field—with instant omniscience (advertising men rely constantly on this habit of ours in their variations on the "testimonial" theme). But the thoughtful reader of an editorial or article of analysis deserves better coin than that.

Third, whether the evidence being offered involves fact, opinion, or both, has an honest summary of the evidence been given to the reader? In making his case, has the analyst made a careful selection of only those items of evidence that support his theme, conveniently overlooking mention of any others? (This is the propagandist's tactic of "deck-stacking.") Or has he drawn up an honest balance sheet and then shown how the weight of evidence is preponderantly on one side?

Fourth, has the writer presented the evidence straight, without doctoring or dilution? Or has he perhaps shifted the terms slightly, so as to make a statistic appear to support something to which it really does not relate? For example, in late 1969 a Gallup Poll report was released in the following news lead:

> PRINCETON, N.J.—President Nixon wins a vote of confidence from 77 percent of Americans on his Vietnam policies among those persons who listened to his Vietnam speech Monday night. Only 6 percent expressed outright opposition to the President's program for ending the Vietnam war, but another 17 percent are undecided.

The next morning an editorial appeared, based largely on the Gallup Poll report in the previous day's news. The editorial began: "There is an unmistakable swell of American public opinion in support of President Nixon's policy of orderly withdrawal of U.S. troops from Vietnam. . . ." And in a later paragraph of the editorial appeared the following: "The Gallup Poll found more than 3 out of every 4 Americans in agreement with the Nixon plan."

On a first, quick reading the editorialist appears to be using a solid piece of evidence, plucked fresh from the news. But the appearance of solidity dissolves at the touch. What the Gallup Poll said was that the president's position was supported by 77 percent of the Americans *who listened to his Vietnam speech Monday night.* That is not the same thing as the editorialist's "more than 3 out of every 4 Americans . . ." since, for one thing, the audience for the speech would have been self-selecting; that is, many more persons favorably disposed toward the president's policies would be listening than would those who were opposed. This sort of "evidence" won't stand up, and the opinion writer who seeks to persuade by the use of such counterfeit will soon lose his credibility—and deservedly.

Evidence, when it is the basis for case making, must be arrayed fairly and solidly, and it must be the genuine article.

Few opinion pieces, however, are based *only* on evidence. Almost all make use of one or more of the devices of argumentation.

BUT HOW MUCH ALIKE?

The editorialist, for example, may use the device of *analogy*. This involves likening one situation to another one and arguing that what can be concluded about the one can also be concluded about the other. Two writers of a textbook on analysis and logic have described the approach:

> Analogy is inference by comparisons. If two things are alike in significant respects, we may infer that they will be alike in another respect. If the Dantscher family finds Newburg a good suburb in which to live, their friends the Maloneys, who have similar tastes and income, ought to find it a good place too. If it costs $14,000 to build a six-room house of given design in Demont, you might estimate that the same house can be built for about $14,000 in another town where costs of labor and materials are approximately the same.
>
> The one test for literal analogy is whether the things or persons compared resemble each other in the most significant respects.[6]

Only, of course, if the resemblance is indeed a true one in the significant respects noted by the two writers will any further comparisons or conclusions be valid. But those further comparisons or conclusions are not *automatically* valid even if the original analogy is a sound one. There is an inferential leap involved. If it is too long a leap for the reader to take, you cannot hope to make your point effectively.[7]

Moreover, even if the resemblance is a true one in significant respects and the inference you want the reader or listener to make is not too much to ask of him, the analogy still may falter. As Chilton R. Bush points out in *Editorial Thinking and Writing,* cited earlier:

The surest clew to a false analogy is the detection of the essential point of difference. In any comparison there are points of resemblance and points of difference, so the soundness of the analogy must rest upon the relative importance of the points of likeness and difference. Whenever some point of difference is so essential that it outweighs the point of resemblance, the analogy, for the purpose of logical proof, is destroyed.[8]

Look back for a moment at the hypothetical case involving the Dantscher and Maloney families and the likelihood that both would find Newburg a pleasant suburb because they have similar tastes and incomes. There is in this an unspoken assumption that the two families are of the same race. But suppose one family is black and the other white and suppose also that the suburb we are discussing is one in which racial tensions persist. Then would both find it equally a pleasant place to live? The one point of difference involved in the comparison would outweigh the points of likeness and destroy the usefulness of the analogy for the purposes of the argument being advanced.

WHO PUSHED THE TRAIN?

Perhaps the commonest form of argumentation in opinion writing is that having to do with cause–effect relationships. A great many editorials or columns, if boiled down to their essence, would be seen to be efforts to establish that X was the cause of Y, or that A will certainly take place sometime soon because B has already happened.

The kind of argument that looks back from an effect now evident and seeks to assign a cause responsible for that effect is a posteriori argument, or argument from effect to cause.

The kind of argument that speculates about the effect an identified cause will produce is a priori argument, or argument from cause to effect.

Let's look at some illustrative examples of such argumentation. Suppose the results are just coming in after a significant presidential primary election. The opinion writers will be looking over the totals and writing pieces contending that the vote went the way it did because, say, one candidate made the wrong kind of public statement at a pivotal point in the campaign, or because the money for TV appearances ran out too soon, or because his rival had more charisma. The analysts have before them an effect—the election returns. Now they are looking back to determine what cause brought about this effect. This would be a form of a posteriori argument.

But now suppose that the election has not yet taken place; the campaign is drawing to a close. The analysts in their columns and editorials are making predictions about the outcome. In so doing they are sorting through a complex of causes they have observed (the various aspects of the campaign) and trying to determine what effect those causes are going to produce come election day. They would be using a form of a priori argument.[9]

Whichever way the argument is laid out, it must advance a sound and defensible causal relationship. Whether the analyst is asserting that the candidate lost because of this or that crucial misstep, or whether he is contending that because the campaign has gone as it has the candidate is likely to lose, the cause–effect link that he is trying to establish must have plausibility and logic. Just because he was leaning on the train as it pulled out of the station, the bystander cannot claim that it was his shove that sent it on its way.

Let's return to the hypothetical primary election. (It's a pretty good example to use because it is not a clear-cut situation; if it were clear-cut, of course, there would be no need to editorialize about it—the matter would be self-explanatory.)

There presumably were numerous factors involved in the campaign. Now that it is over no one—not even the loftily omniscient editorial writer—can be entirely certain which factors were of crucial significance in the minds of the voters. Yet the editorialist wants to write something that will be helpful to reader understanding. To do that he will need to sort through the various forces and factors of the campaign as painstakingly as he can in order to determine as nearly as possible which ones had a significant effect. Anyone can guess. The editorialist must do more than that. He must sift through the evidence and build a persuasive case for his explanation of what happened and why.

If there are reliable opinion-poll figures for various dates during the campaign, he may have some benchmarks to work with. When did shifts in voter sentiment take place? To what events or developments were they keyed in time? Is it likely that these shifts in voter attitude were *causally* related to the developments as well as *temporally* related to them? Were there other factors that might have been significant, though unseen?

How do the two candidates and their advisers analyze the outcome? How much should their analyses be discounted as being either self-serving or rationalized? What issues seemed to be uppermost in the voters' minds, to judge by, say, letters to the editor during the campaign? And how representative are these outcroppings?

As the editorialist tries to build his case, assigning causes that in his judgment have produced the effect now in view, he needs to muster convincing evidence and draw on seasoned insight in order to establish a believable causal link, one that stands the test of analysis and challenge. Since his case will have to rest in part on speculation, the reputation he has been able to establish for soundness and credibility will have a good deal to do with the effectiveness of his argument.

TESTING CAUSE-EFFECT ARGUMENTATION

For the very reason that at least some of his case must be based on insight and educated guesswork, the editorialist cannot often make use of scientific tests to be sure that his causal reasoning is sound. But it is important that he be familiar with some of these tests, particularly two of John Stuart Mill's canons. The textbook on logic mentioned earlier, *From Fact to Judgment,* summarizes the two well:

> Mill's canon of *agreement* warns that there must be one and *only one* antecedent which always precedes the phenomenon if we are to ascribe it as the cause. If two or more antecedents always precede the phenomenon, then we will not know which had the influence. The perfect formula would look like this:
> A, B, C, and D are the only antecedents of R (the Result).
> A, F, C, and G are the only antecedents of R (another instance).
> B, K, C, and L are the only antecedents of R (another instance).
> In these three instances, C is the only antecedent which always precedes R; hence C must be a necessary antecedent and hence the cause of R. It is either "the cause, or an indispensable part of the cause," to use Mill's own words.
> . . . *Method of Difference.* This second of Mill's Canons says in effect: Here a thing happens, and there it doesn't. What's the difference in the two situations? If we find a single point of difference—a single difference among the antecedents—there we have "the cause." Now the perfect formula would look this way:
> A, B, C, and D are the only antecedents of R (the Result).
> A, B, C, and D occur and we get R
> A, B, and D occur and we do not get R
> C is here the only point of difference; hence it must be an essential part of the cause. [10]

As the authors point out, Mill's canons are most useful in the scientific setting, where controlled experiments can be performed. Not often does the editorialist find himself with a situation susceptible to such control. He can make use of the canons as aids to his own thinking and reasoning, however, even if he cannot directly apply them to very many of the situations that he may wish to analyze.

HELP FROM THE RESEARCHERS

The opinion writer can draw profitably on the thinking not only of logicians but also of communication theorists as he goes about the business of making persuasive cases.

We have already noted in an earlier chapter that the findings of research have some bearing on the intuitive feeling of many editorial writers that they must not get too far ahead of their readers. The researchers point out that an individual uses *selective perception* as he attends to messages directed at him, paying attention to those that conform to the receiver's view of the world and avoiding those that are dissonant or incongruous—that is, ones that suggest a picture of the world that is very unlike the one the receiver has been accustomed to accept. There is scientifically supported reason, then, to backstop the editorialist's intuitive conviction that he should stay within hailing distance of his audience.

A good many other findings of communication research can be of use to the opinion writer as he tries to devise ways to reach and persuade his readers or viewers. Sometimes these findings reinforce commonsense assumptions; sometimes they suggest unexpected amendments to those assumptions.

For example, the point has several times been made earlier in this book that an opinion writer must have established a good reputation with his audience if he hopes to have his case-making efforts accepted. Much research confirms that messages from a high-credibility or well-accepted source will be more effective than those from a low-credibility source. But there are a couple of interesting modifications to this general rule.

One study produced findings suggesting that there may not always be such an advantage to the high-credibility persuader. Over a period of time, the receiver of the message tends to forget the source, but continues to remember the *substance* of the argument and to modify his own views as a result. This "sleeper effect" may mean that the opinion writer can hope to have some impact even on a hostile audience if he makes a memorable enough case. [11]

Another set of researchers discovered that even when a source is considered by the audience to be of low credibility, his message may nevertheless seem persuasive to that audience if he is making an argument that runs *counter to his own interests.* In other words, if you are a columnist noted for a strongly liberal orientation but you write a column commending the program of a conservative candidate, you may have a persuasive effect even on readers who would ordinarily be inclined to discount your views automatically.[12]

These two sidelights do not, of course, vitiate the basic premise that the would-be persuader will have a better chance of achieving his goal if the audience thinks of him as reliable and authoritative than if it has a negative posture toward him. But they may be useful bits of information to tuck away for use in special circumstances.

ONE SIDE OR TWO?

A more consistently significant finding developed through a series of research studies has to do with the question of whether a persuasive case ought to include only those arguments that point toward the desired conclusion or whether it ought instead to acknowledge the existence of both (or all) sides and then go on to argue for one of them.

Numerous studies have sought to determine which approach—one-sided or two-sided—is more effective in terms of attitude change. They boil down to the following conclusions:

1. For persons who are already favorably disposed toward the point of view of the communicator, the one-sided presentation is more effective than the two-sided. If the target audience is already pretty well in your camp, bringing up opposing arguments may only have the effect of arousing doubts and weakening the predisposition.
2. For persons who have a limited education, the one-sided approach is more effective than the two-sided approach.[13]

What does this mean for the opinion writer?

It means, for one thing, that if he is trying to reach a poorly educated audience that already agrees with his point of view, he can make a one-sided case, ignoring the existence of opposing points. (The mass media opinion writer is rarely in this position.)

But if he wants to reach a relatively well-educated audience that includes persons who do not at this stage accept the point of view he is trying to advance, he had better plan on putting the whole situation before his readers or listeners. He should acknowledge the arguments opposed to his view and try to muster evidence and argumentation to counter their effect and reinforce his own case. But he cannot afford to finesse those opposition arguments, pretend they don't exist. For he knows that the target he must aim for is the thoughtful reader, the opinion leader who pays a good deal of attention to the mass media and knows that most issues are not one-sided.

The propagandist is likely to try to get away with the one-sided, stacked-deck approach; the opinion writer cannot risk it.

There may also be a dividend for the opinion writer who uses the two-sided approach. Not only does it give him a better chance of persuading the thoughtful reader or listener the first time around; it may also give him the chance to *inoculate* his audience against the opposing arguments so that those arguments will have little or no effect if they are later encountered in another communication.

If the editorialist admits the existence of the opposition's side of the case, but then goes on to point out its weaknesses, it may well be that his audience will acquire an immunity to the blandishments of the other side. If, on the other hand, he presents only his own side and pretends the other side doesn't exist, the audience may be quite willing to give that other side a hearing when it finally does come up in some other paper or some other broadcast. (Incidentally, this form of inoculation of an audience—by bringing up the opposing arguments and then undercutting them as completely as possible—is far more effective than another inoculative approach, that of name calling. Simply attacking the other side and impugning the motives of those who take that position may to some extent discredit the opposition in the eyes of the audience, but not so much so as refutation of the opposing *arguments*.)[14]

GET THEM INTO THE ACT

Another useful contribution of the communication researchers is their finding that the effectiveness of an effort at attitude change is greater if the target audience can somehow be made to take an active rather than a passive role. This has been found to be particularly noticeable in situations involving role-playing, group discussion, or sensitivity training. But for the opinion writer it also has some application. The editorialist who can somehow get his audience involved in the case-making discussion (by responding to a built-in quiz or a series of questions) or who can build his persuasive article to a climax that calls for a positive response (such as writing a letter to a congressman or returning an opinion ballot to the paper) can expect that the impact of his efforts will be reinforced by this involvement.[15]

Obviously, not every editorial or magazine essay can wind up with a ringing call for the reader to rush to his desk to dash off a letter; the mail service is clogged enough already. Also, there is a point of diminishing return with such techniques. They can be used once in a while with profit, but repetition stales. Nevertheless the opinion writer ought to seize any chances that come his way to bring about some positive involvement of the reader or viewer; it represents a proven way to enhance a persuasive appeal and prolong its effect.

DON'T LEAVE TOO MANY BLANKS

Somewhat related to the last point is another research finding dealing with the degree to which a persuader ought to spell out the specific conclusions he hopes that his audience will accept.

Should he unfold his reasoning and then put the conclusion bluntly and explicitly? Or should he draw his audience along on a trail of irresistible evidence and logic, confident that at the end he can leave the listener or reader to take the last step himself?

There are variations in the results of research studies, but most of them seem to point to the explicit approach as the more effective one. If the opinion writer leads the reader down the path, but doesn't point out the final step in specific terms, there is always the chance that some members of the audience won't perceive which way they are supposed to go—or that some others will be too lazy to make the final spurt on their own. The persuader's chances appear to be better if he makes it plain what conclusions he hopes his audience will draw from the discussion that he has developed.[16]

FIRST OR LAST?

On another question of strategy—how to order one's arguments in a persuasive communication—the findings of the communication theorists are not so clear-cut. As one scholar summarizes the situation:

> Should one begin with his best point, or build up to it? Here the evidence seems to be conflicting. Hovland, Janis, and Kelley have suggested two apparently sound and useful propositions, however. Where the audience is familiar with the subject, and deep concern is felt over it, then, they suggest, there seems to be good reason for climax order—that is, for leading up to the main point at the end. On the other hand, if the audience is unfamiliar with the subject, or uninterested, there may be good reason to

introduce the main point first. By so doing, the communicator will be most likely to gain the audience's attention and interest.[17]

In this chapter we have inventoried some ways of argumentation and case making and have noted also the findings of communication researchers that offer useful assists to the opinion writer as he approaches his task of building the heart of the editorial article.

It should be apparent that nothing like a pat or universal formula has emerged from the discussion. The opinion writer must proceed from case to case, choosing the techniques and the approaches that best suit his purposes in each. And when he has finished constructing his case, he ought to step back a pace or two and give the finished product a careful last check to be sure that everything worked out as he had intended. We will consider that process in the next chapter.

NOTES

1. John L. Hulteng, "Back-Door Editorializing," *Nieman Reports,* January 1950, p. 9.

2. McGinnis, Joseph, *The Selling of the President, 1968,* New York, Trident Press, 1969.

3. The foregoing discussion is adapted from Daniel Katz, "The Functional Approach to the Study of Attitudes," in *Reader in Public Opinion and Communication,* edited by Bernard Berelson and Morris Janowitz, New York, Free Press, 1966, pp. 51–64.

4. From Roscoe Drummond's syndicated column written for publication on July 20, 1971.

5. Hal Liston, "First Be A Little More Humble," *Masthead,* Summer 1971, p. 45.

6. Harold F. Graves and Bernard S. Oldsey, *From Fact to Judgment,* New York, Macmillan, 1957, p. 172.

7. It should be borne in mind that what is being discussed is *literal analogy,* a device of argumentation that seeks to make literal comparisons. This should not be confused with *figurative analogy,* an illustrative device such as simile and metaphor, in which the comparisons suggested are not intended to be taken literally.

8. Chilton R. Bush, *Editorial Thinking and Writing,* New York, Appleton, 1932, p. 159.

9. An a priori argument need not always relate to a future event, of course. As Bush points out (*Editorial Thinking and Writing,* p. 105): "Arguments from cause to effect may argue from the present to the future, from the past to the future, from the past to the present, or

from the past to a less remote past. In any instance, however, the argument is that the circumstances are, *by their nature,* such as to produce the disputed effect."

10. Graves and Oldsey, *op. cit.,* pp. 175–176.

11. This is discussed more fully in Carl I. Hovland and Walter Weiss, "The Influence of Source Credibility on Communication Effectiveness," in Berelson and Janowitz, *op. cit.,* pp. 275–288.

12. See Vernon A. Stone and Harrogadde S. Eswara, "Likeability and Self-Interest of the Source of Attitude Change," *Journalism Quarterly,* Spring 1969, pp. 61–68.

13. For a complete discussion, see C. I. Hovland, A. A. Lumsdaine, and F. D. Sheffield, "The Effect of Presenting 'One Side' vs. 'Both Sides' in Changing Opinions on a Controversial Subject," in Berelson and Janowitz, *op. cit.,* pp. 261–274.

14. See Vernon A. Stone, "Individual Differences and Inoculation Against Persuasion," *Journalism Quarterly,* Summer 1969, pp. 267–273.

15. Marvin Karlins and Herbert I. Abelson, *Persuasion,* New York, Springer Publishing Co., 1970, pp. 19–21.

16. *Ibid.,* pp. 11–14.

17. Wilbur Schramm, *The Process and Effects of Mass Communication,* Urbana, University of Illinois Press, 1965, p. 14.

8
Pitfalls and Pratfalls

There are so many reasons why the opinion writer wants to avoid, if at all possible, going out on the street or out on the air with egg on his face. The opinion section is the showcase of the publication; the deadlines are more relaxed, so the quality of writing ought to be better than elsewhere in the paper or magazine; the audience is not necessarily favorably disposed to accept the intellectual massage of the opinion writer, so it must be deft and painless; and the critics are lying in ambush by platoons, ready to rush forward with the triumphant correction or the savagely effective counter-thrust.

So the work of the opinion writer should be as carefully crafted as a Swiss watch, smooth running, and with no chinks anywhere in the casing. When he puts an argument together the writer should be sure that every linkage is solid, every transition effortless, and every word, phrase, or allusion chosen to convey precisely the right effect. That's a large order. Sometimes the editorialist falls short in filling it.

He may fall short in a variety of ways. It is beyond the scope of this book, or any book, to catalog all those ways and educate the would-be opinion writer to avoid them. But there are some kinds of flaws that are lamentably frequent, and it is worth taking up some space to identify these and post a large, red warning flag on each.

IF A LITTLE IS GOOD, A LOT MAY BE TOO MUCH

One of these flaws that particularly needs to be flagged is *rhetorical overkill*. A great many editorials are marred, sometimes fatally, by the writer's inability to control his flow of words. He may go along well for a time, crafting a strongly persuasive argument built on evidence and logic, and then suddenly blow it, boiling over in a gush of angry verbiage that leaves the reader snickering rather than convinced.

Consider an example. A newspaper editorialist put together an effective piece criticizing a group of militants who had noisily disrupted a speech on the campus of a nearby university. He marshalled his points ably, acknowledging the motives of the disrupters but taking issue with their tactics. Then, in the closing paragraph, he couldn't quite keep his cool. He wound up the editorial with these lines:

> Thus, on Monday, the mottoed wind of freedom did not blow at _____ University. The foul wind that did blow gagged academic freedom and sent fairness reeling, nauseated by the stink of an awful halitosis of the political soul.

Presumably a good many of his readers also went reeling away from that wild flourish, the earlier arguments forgotten in the impression created by the ludicrous extravagance of the closing passage.

Certainly the editorialist sometimes must let his anger show; but it should be a disciplined and controlled anger. It should not be permitted to offset the careful buildup of logic and reason that may also be a part of the opinion piece.

"NOT EVEN THE QUESTION ITSELF . . ."

But there is danger in the opposite extreme, too, in what might be called underkill, or *excessive detachment.* Some opinion writers make it a point to stand so far back from the subject, and view it with so exquisitely dispassionate a viewpoint, that their contribution, if any, can barely be detected by the reader.

Karl E. Meyer, himself an editorial writer, pointed up this hazard effectively in his book *The New America:*[1]

> The traditional argument for free speech, as formulated by John Stuart Mill, assumed that the collision of strong opinion provided the best mechanism for arriving at the truth. The beneficiary of hard-hitting controversy, Mill contended, was not the impassioned participant but "the calmer and more disinterested bystander." Mill was less concerned by the violent conflicts of parts of the truth than by the quiet suppression of half of it, because "there is always hope when people are forced to listen to both sides; it is when they attend to one that errors harden into prejudice and truth itself ceases to have the effect of truth, by being exaggerated into falsehood."

So reasoned Mill; surely he would be troubled by a tradition of political commentary which seeks to express the consensus rather than criticize it. No matter how fair-minded the new school of pundits may be, their excessive emphasis on detachment may—paradoxically—prejudice the broader purpose of discovering the truth. There is a maxim by G. K. Chesterton which puts the matter astringently: "The angry historians see one side of the question. The calm historians see nothing at all, not even the question itself."

THE COSTLY SLUR

A third pitfall into which opinion writers are tempted to fall is that of *irrelevant personal attack*. Please note the qualifying adjective "irrelevant," for there are many occasions when the editorialist intentionally and properly mounts a personal attack—on a dilatory bureaucrat, a venal official, a demagogic candidate. In such instances, the personal character or individual behavior of the writer's target may be altogether relevant to the subject under discussion.

But on other occasions the opinion writer may take a swing in passing at someone or something mentioned in an editorial when personal character or individual behavior are not at all the issue (such as the columnists' sneers at President Nixon's penchant for ketchup on cottage cheese). In the logician's terms, this would be using *ad hominem* argument, attacking the man instead of the issue; in the catalog of propaganda devices it would be labeled *name calling*. In any case, the use of *irrelevant* personal attack by an opinion writer can backfire disastrously.

Again, let's take an example. A metropolitan newspaper took editorial note of a demonstration that had been staged in the city outside a courtroom in which a meeting of the Federal Subversive Activities Control Board was being held. The editorial acknowledged that the board and its activities were by now perhaps archaic and that the law establishing the agency probably should be repealed. But then the writer observed, almost as an aside to his main theme:

> Picketing by scores of largely stringy-haired, bearded, unkempt college students is not likely to convince many persons that the law is bad. If such persons are for repeal, most observers quite likely would conclude, it should be retained.

Within a couple of days the letters-to-the-editor column of the newspaper was clogged with angry reactions to the editorial—but scarcely one of them made any mention of the chief burden of the piece. Virtually all of them focused on the single short paragraph quoted above. The gratuitous slur had arrested the attention of the readers and all of the writer's careful examination of the issue of the validity of the control board and its authorizing legislation was ignored.

Some sample excerpts from the letters suggest how completely this shift of emphasis had taken place:

From one writer:

> There is no need to go to such lengths to point out the physical appearance of these students. I am sure that if the demonstration had been made up of ladies from the Daughters of the American Revolution there would have been no such emphasis on clothes, hair styles, and "skin problems".

And another:

> One wonders if the issue would have provoked as much newspaper coverage or editorial comment on your pages without this picketing. It would seem that we owe these young people a vote of thanks for bringing this issue to the attention of the public.

And still one more:

> All hail that greasy kid stuff! Have your clean-shaven, non-stringy-haired and frivolous reporters forgotten that Abraham Lincoln had a (gasp) beard? And what about the Good Samaritan? Not only a beard, but sandals yet. How un-American.

The lesson for the would-be opinion writer is plain enough: Don't leave any handholds—most particularly irrelevant personal attacks—that critics can use to overturn all of the rest of your painstakingly structured effort or as an excuse to bypass and ignore it altogether.

AS EVERYONE KNOWS . . .

Begging the question is something of which everyone is often guilty. It involves assuming the truth of a premise that actually is still being debated and then going on to build a structure of argument founded on this yet unproven premise.

The opinion writer must constantly confront the temptation to sprinkle unproven premises throughout his work. And if he doesn't have enough character to resist that temptation he had better look for work on some specialized publication aimed at the already converted.

In this era of accelerating change and culture shock few precepts have either permanence or widespread acceptance. There are minority groups who are challenging the "writing it white" syndrome of the mass media (the tendency to assume that all readers or all viewers are white and to treat all news on a "we-them" basis). There are women's liberation advocates ready to attack the ingrained pattern of thought that uses "any man," "mankind," or "the nation's manpower" as routine and universal expressions. Any opinion writer soon discovers that he cannot get away with begging the question on a controversial issue, whatever its nature.

The editorialist who studs his copy with such phrases as "most observers quite likely would conclude" (that's from the editorial quoted in the last section) ought to pause a moment to consider whether this is really the case or whether he in fact means "*this observer* would conclude."

And the editorialist who attempts to glide over an assumption that may be hotly debatable in the eyes of many of his readers will at once have problems on his hands. One editorial writer concluded a piece on the trend to phase out ROTC courses on the nation's campuses with the following:

> There is only one sound reason for wanting to damage the ROTC program. That is to weaken and confuse the military at a time when it is engaged in its greatest struggle in almost a quarter century.

Here, in 37 words, the writer had, in effect, begged *two* questions. Implicit in his comment was the assumption that the military was engaged in a great struggle for which the nation should and would offer support; that struggle was the Vietnam War, and the national anguish over its legitimacy was at its height at the time. Also built into the writer's thesis was the assumption that those seeking to eliminate ROTC programs from the campus had only one motivation—to weaken the military; that point, too, was the subject of energetic debate.

Another writer, proposing that service in the Peace Corps be made the basis for exemption from the draft, wrote:

> There is a war being waged around the world right now; it is a war against hunger, sickness, and ignorance. This is the war which members of the Peace Corps have carried to foreign shores.

When these youths wage their battles, they are doing as much for the United States and the world as any U.S. soldier who ever carried a rifle. For this reason we feel that work in the Peace Corps should exempt an individual from serving in the military forces of this country.

In this instance the writer begged a very central question—is service in the Peace Corps truly equivalent to the risking of one's life in battle? Unless he confronted that question and somehow resolved it for the reader who had a son then serving in battle, the editorial would not jell. In this case the writer never did touch on the central question, contenting himself with gliding by it in those opening lines, and as a result the editorial made no solid impact with its main thesis.

A USEFUL TOOL

Flawed logic or faulty strategy can show up in an opinion piece without the writer realizing it. Preoccupied with his thesis, the editorialist builds away, block on block, without sensing that somewhere along the way he has left a structural weakness that makes the whole edifice vulnerable.

For that reason, the opinion writer ought to cultivate the habit of bench testing his finished work before committing it to print or to the air. He should check over the logic in his article, just as the precision-tool maker checks the tolerance of his product to be sure that it will do the job for which it is intended.

In the previous chapter it was suggested that any argument from analogy ought to be analyzed to guard against the presence of some crucial, invalidating aspect of difference that might destroy the effectiveness of the comparison. It was also suggested that cause–effect argumentation be subjected to scrutiny to make sure that the linkages are all plausible and well secured.

In addition to this kind of "eyeballing" to detect errors as he goes about building his line of argument, the opinion writer can also make use of a specific testing tool—the syllogism—to check out the validity of his case after he has finished putting it together.

The syllogism is a pattern for expressing the essence of an argument in stripped-down terms so that its basic characteristics can be evaluated. It consists of three parts:

1. A major premise, which is typically a general rule that is universally accepted.

2. A minor premise, which is usually a specific instance or case that is included within the general rule of the major premise.
3. A conclusion, which in some way relates the major and minor premises, usually by applying the general rule to the specific case.

A simple syllogism might be:

Major premise: All dogs normally have four legs.
Minor premise: My pet, Sparky, is a dog.
Conclusion: Therefore, Sparky has four legs.

Now, setting aside the aberrant and unhappy possibility that Sparky may have been born deformed or may have lost a leg in an accident, this syllogism represents sound deduction.   The major premise is generally accepted, the minor premise is a provable assertion, and the conclusion flows logically from the expressed relationship between the first two elements.

Suppose, however, that the syllogism had been set up thus:

Major premise: All dogs bark.
Minor premise: My pet, Sparky, is a dog.
Conclusion: Therefore, Sparky barks.

In this instance the major premise is open to challenge. There are some breeds of dogs (the Basenji, for one) that do not bark. The chain of reasoning thus becomes suspect.

Or suppose the syllogism had been:

Major premise: Most pets are either dogs or cats.
Minor Premise: I have a pet named Pokey.
Conclusion: Therefore, Pokey must be either a dog or a cat.

As it happens, Pokey is a parakeet, and the syllogism is faulty. In this instance, the major premise is true enough, and so is the minor premise. But the minor premise does not represent a case included within the general rule of the major premise, and thus the sequence of argument once again breaks down; the conclusion is illogical.

For the syllogistic format to hold, the major premise must be true; the minor premise must also be true and in addition must be embraced within the general rule of the major premise; and the conclusion must relate the first two elements logically, with no shifting of terms.

For the opinion writer, the syllogism can be a versatile and useful tool for testing his reasoning. When he has finished his editorial or column he can extract from it the core of argument, arrange it in syllogistic form, and see whether it holds together.

Let's look at an example based on an actual editorial, slightly para-phrased to mask the identity of the paper involved but otherwise just as it was published:

> Students at Harvard, Illinois, and Minnesota have been protest-ing the appearance on their campuses of recruiters for a chemical company. The company, it seems, makes napalm, which is very naughty.
>
> But as it happens the company is also working with a firm in India to produce peanut flour. This flour could go a long way not only to stem India's famine, but also to correct the protein defi-ciency that afflicts so many of India's people.
>
> It's too bad that students at Harvard, Illinois, and Minnesota care so little about famine in India.

As is often the case when one uses a real-life example instead of a textbook case, reducing this editorial to syllogistic terms is somewhat difficult. In fact, about three different syllogisms might be constructed on the basis of those three brief paragraphs.

One of them might be this:

Major premise: If you do a good thing, this offsets your doing a bad thing.

Minor premise: The chemical company makes peanut flour, which is good, and also makes napalm, which is bad.

Conclusion: Therefore, the company's creditable action offsets its discreditable action, and it should not be subjected to criticism.

If that, indeed, is one strand of the editorial's argumentation, there are some flaws in it. The major premise is obviously open to challenge; it is not a general rule that is universally accepted. The minor premise may also be vulnerable in that it appears to equate elements that may be very unlike in qualitative terms (is a criminal's guilt offset by the fact that he has always been good to his mother?).

But that is not the only way in which the editorial writer's argument could be construed. Another possible syllogistic distillation of the piece might be this:

Major premise: Persons concerned about prevention of famine would not criticize a firm engaged in making a product that would ease famine problems.

Minor premise: The chemical company that is being criticized by student protestors is making a product, peanut flour, that would stem India's famine.

Conclusion: Therefore the student protestors are indifferent to famine in India.

If you accept this as the editorialist's chief line of argument, you discover that it, too, is in trouble. The major premise is not necessarily universally true on its face. Too many unstated variables might be involved. And if the major premise will not hold, neither will the remainder of the syllogism.

The reader may want to try his hand at constructing yet another syllogistic interpretation of the editorial's argument; others are possible. But he will have difficulty finding *any* version that will stand up to the syllogism test. (Incidentally, this same editorial might be faulted on another point. Is "naughty" the appropriate term to use in conjunction with napalm, the substance used in military bombs?)

During the late 1960s and early 1970s a frequently encountered editorial theme, in newspapers, magazines, and on broadcasting channels, was that such campus groups as the Students for a Democratic Society must be Communist-directed because they were demanding unilateral American withdrawal from Vietnam, just as were the propaganda spokesmen for Hanoi and Peking. Anyone who took the trouble to reduce such an argument to syllogistic form would have been able to spot its weakness at once.

This is how the thesis boils down:

Major premise: Anyone who advocates unilateral American withdrawal from Vietnam is either Communist or Communist directed.

Minor premise: Members of Students for a Democratic Society advocate unilateral American withdrawal from Vietnam.

Conclusion: Therefore, members of Students for a Democratic Society are either Communists or Communist directed.

Before this chain of argument can be made to hold together, the major premise must be defended as true and universally accepted, which would be impossible to do except with certain highly selected audiences.

Regular use of the syllogistic test by opinion writers might be as useful as the conference system in preventing faulty logic from finding its way into print and on the air. While the conference approach provides a check on error or flawed reasoning at the beginning of the process, the bench test serves the same purpose at the end of the line.

FINDING WEAK SPOTS

The syllogism can, however, be useful somewhere in the middle as well. Suppose an editorialist has devised in his mind an editorial thesis that runs something like this: The United States should not invest billions in an antiballistic-missile system that would be capable of intercepting only part of the intercontinental and other missiles that would be directed against us in the event of an all-out atomic attack.

Before he begins putting the editorial together, he might strip down the line of argument to syllogistic form, just to see how it looks. It might come out this way:

Major premise: It would be wrong to spend billions on any defense system that would stop only part of the attacking missiles.

Minor premise: The planned antiballistic-missile system would stop only part of the attacking missiles we could expect in all-out war.

Conclusion: Therefore, it would be wrong to spend billions on this ABM system.

Just in the process of distilling the line of argument the writer can see that he is going to have some problems in building the editorial.

In the first place, he must be prepared to make a persuasive case for the major premise of his line of argument; it is debatable as it stands (if the lives of only half the population could be saved, wouldn't it still be worth billions?).

Second, he can see that his case will also depend on mustering evidence to support the minor premise—that the planned system would stop only part of the missiles. Presumably he can bring expert witnesses into the box for this purpose.

Because he has taken the precaution to set up his basic line of argumentation in syllogistic form in advance, the writer has been alerted to the kind of job he must do in building the editorial. Without the preliminary check, he might have worked half the day writing a piece that, when finished, would be so full of holes he would have to junk it and start over. The syllogistic bench test is an indispensable aid to the opinion writer, both as time-saver and face-saver.

There are, of course, some editorials that cannot easily be reduced to syllogistic form for the purpose of analysis—or at least they cannot be reduced to the particular form that we have been discussing up to now, the *categorical syllogism.* In such cases one of the other syllogistic forms may prove useful as a testing instrument.

These other forms include the *disjunctive syllogism,* which is set up thus:

Major premise: All humans are either male or female.
Minor premise: Francis, a human, is not a female.
Conclusion: Therefore, Francis is a male.

If you make use of this syllogistic form you must be sure that the major premise is true and inclusive. (In the above example, some clinical quibblers might provide a challenge.)

There is also the *hypothetical syllogism,* an example of which might be:

Major premise: If prices go up, the public will buy fewer goods.
Minor premise: Prices are going up.
Conclusion: Therefore, the public will soon cut back purchases of goods.

The use of this syllogistic form involves testing for the various fallacies and weaknesses described in connection with the categorical syllogism, but there is an additional problem as well. The hypothetical major premise, simply because it is hypothetical, provides a somewhat less dependable underpinning for the structure of reasoning than in the case of the categorical syllogism. Is the conditional generalization embodied in the major premise one that has been proven by repeated test, one that is universally accepted? In the example cited, *is* it always the case that if prices go up the public will buy less? On a rising market, with expectation of still further increases in prospect, wouldn't it be possible that a price rise might bring about *heavier* buying (for hoarding) rather than less?

A good many editorial themes do involve a line of reasoning that can be summarized in the form of the hypothetical syllogism, and their weaknesses can be identified in time if the writer takes the few extra minutes involved in going through the bench-test process.[2]

NOTES

1. Karl E. Meyer, *The New America*, New York, Basic Books, 1961, pp. 114–115.

2. A fuller discussion of the several forms of the syllogism, and the various fallacies associated with them, may be found in either Chilton R. Bush, *Editorial Thinking and Writing*, Appleton, New York, 1932, pp. 170–181, or Harold F. Graves and Bernard S. Oldsey, *From Fact to Judgment*, New York, Macmillan, 1957, pp. 166–169.

9
At the Typewriter

Most of the burden of this book has to do with the devising of policy, the identification of editorial ideas, and the construction of a persuasive line of argumentation. The emphasis is appropriate, for these are the *distinctive aspects* of the opinion function. Editorial *writing,* as writing, is in many respects not greatly different from other forms of journalistic expression.

Nevertheless, there are some points to be noted about the writing of opinion pieces—points related to tactics, structure, or style—that would not necessarily be familiar to students who have already acquired background and experience as news or feature writers.

Let's consider first the matter of style.

BLANDNESS AND JARGON

We have noted earlier in this book that editorial style should not be ornate, or top-heavy with obscure allusions and a polysyllabic vocabulary. Instead, it ought to be clear, precise, pointed, and capable of being understood by most of the members of the audience to which it is directed (since the opinion writer for any mass medium cannot be sure exactly which members of that audience are the influentials he hopes to reach).

Yet this ideal prescription is not always met on a good many editorial pages, even the most highly regarded ones. Henry Fairlie, a British correspondent stationed in America, once offered his appraisal of some of this country's leading newspapers. Of the *New York Times,* he said: "No other of the newspapers I am discussing labours so prodigiously or so unsuccessfully, to make clear what it is trying to say. Apart from

James Reston, its editorial page is the most unintelligible in either country."[1]

He went on in similar vein about a number of other American papers. Of only one did he have any good words to say:

> Of all the newspapers, American and British, which I am discussing, the *Wall Street Journal* is the only one which, with intelligence, polemic, candour, and wit, continually questions the way in which the world is going. . . . The lesson, I believe, is one of general application. Newspapers cannot be really forceful, cannot even be really illuminating, in their editorial comment if they lack intellectual conviction and passion, if they are content (as most of them are) simply to differ a little, while swimming along in the "mainstream."[2]

Fairlie's comments constitute a severe indictment of what he regarded as the blandness and vapidity of opinion writing, even taking into consideration his friendly bow to the *Journal.* Is the indictment a fair one?

It is perhaps too sweeping to be fair. He generalized his observations on the basis of a few newspapers; and he applied British standards, which tend to place a higher premium on literary quality than do standards generally observed in this country.

Nonetheless, some of his points cannot easily be set aside. For one thing, he is close to the mark when he categorizes opinion writing in American newspapers as "swimming along in the 'mainstream.' "

We have noted in Chapter 4 some of the factors involved in the development of policy; they tend to bring about more blandness than fire in the editorial columns, admittedly. There *is* a temptation to stay safely in the mainstream, close to the positions held by most of the readers, rather than provide dramatic leadership.

And as to the unintelligibility for which Fairlie particularly criticizes the *New York Times,* that, too, is uncomfortably prevalent in much opinion writing. Not on all editorial pages, to be sure; some crackle with crisp and lucid prose. But others lean too much on a special jargon of the trade, an "editorialese" that is concocted of vague phrases, ambiguous expressions, and high-sounding but empty rhetoric. Editorialese represents a specialized language for avoiding flat, clear statements of position, and it can be recognized at a glance once you get the hang of it.

Creed C. Black, then managing editor of the *Chicago Daily News,* once put together a composite editorial made up of such phrasing plucked out of a dozen editorial pages in two days:

The Need For Leadership

The Blank report presents an opportunity for further thoughtful re-examination. This carefully and thoughtfully considered proposal has been in the making for eight months. During this gestation period all segments of public interest have been represented and heeded.

The current report adds weight to the previous findings.

On the other hand, we have something new.

Honest men may differ in answering these questions. But the problems must not block progress. The time has come for leadership on this long-overdue reform.

It is a frightening prospect. What is being done to meet the acute situation should have been done long ago because the crisis was foreseen.

Bluntly put, some intelligent taxpayers are getting fed up with this kind of performance. Whether that will be effective in this case is problematical.

It is delusive to pretend that success will come easily. Disrespect for constituted authority is widespread. But something must be done. The only question now is how to go about it. Not to do so is deliberately to flout the public interest.

The time for action is now.[3]

Black's clip-and-paste effort, drawing on the actual phrasing of editorials he had read, represents as devastating a comment on the quality of American opinion writing as Fairlie's frontal attack.

But both critics are of course exaggerating to make their points, and their views must be considered in perspective. The *Wall Street Journal* does indeed have a fine editorial page, but it is not the only publication in which there is lucid and forceful editorial style, as some of the examples cited later on will illustrate. And as for the blandness that so disturbs the observer from Britain, even that is not quite so universal as he suggests. As evidence, consider the excerpts below from an editorial in the *San Francisco Chronicle,* which bristle with enough polemic and passion to satisfy even Mr. Fairlie. The editorial was occasioned by the action of another San Francisco newspaper, the *Examiner,* which had just announced that it would no longer accept advertising from theaters or movie houses where pornographic films or shows were being presented. Here's a sample of the *Chronicle's* reaction, which was presented in a full-column editorial:

It is a melancholy experience to witness the spectacle of a newspaper recanting its journalistic faith in the public square. . . .

The incident to which we have reference is an editorial that appeared in The San Francisco Examiner two days ago, in which the editors announced, with the grandiloquent rhetoric of a junior college dropout, that they would no longer accept any advertisements whatsoever pertaining to the so-called stag, or pornographic, or blue movies that have grown like mushrooms in a number of dark, fetid San Francisco "theatres."

In the event that some of our readers may have missed this gloomy milestone of journalism, we are herewith reprinting the subject editorial in the adjoining columns.

The fact that the policy-makers on The San Francisco Examiner find these motion picture exhibitions to be less than savory is perfectly understandable and natural and is to be commended, although the existence of such films is not exactly news.

What is utterly disturbing is the fact that a newspaper of even moderate daily circulation should debase the coinage of the American free press by refusing to print advertising for these woebegone enterprises without even looking at or considering the merit of the actual advertisement.

Textually, the reprinted essay is journalistic dung.

It is a spattering of chicken droppings on the printed pages of man's magnificent achievement in developing our written language.

After these advertisements have been flatly censored out of its columns, we wonder what the *Examiner* will turn to next?

Will it delete automobile advertising because large numbers of people are killed by motor vehicles every day?[4]

And so on, in similar vein, for another half column.

Overkill? *Ad hominem?* Maybe so. But certainly not bland. And a reminder that any all-encompassing categorization of American editorial style is probably inappropriate. Considering the various forms that opinion writing takes in the mass media—newspaper editorials, columns, magazine essays, broadcast editorials—it would be fairer to say that there is a whole spectrum of editorial style. We will note examples from various points on that stylistic spectrum, some good and some bad, as we continue the discussion on the specifics of opinion writing.

PLURAL AND FACELESS

So far as editorial writing in newspapers and some magazines is concerned, there are a couple of conventions of style that are all but universal. And they are ones that often prove bothersome and mystifying to the reader.

One involves the use of the *editorial we,* and the other is the fact that most newspaper and magazine editorial writing is unsigned.

The reason for both usages is the same—the opinion expression set out in the editorial page of the newspaper or magazine is intended to be perceived as that of the publication as a whole, not of an individual writer. Thus it is unsigned, faceless. Thus, also, the frequent use of "we" when the writer wants to use a first-person reference in his writing. The we stands for the board of editors, the policy makers of the publication, and underlines the fact that the editorial is not being offered simply as the view of one person, as is the case with the syndicated column.

Broadcast editorials are of course not faceless in the sense that they are delivered by a voice, or a televised individual. Yet even then the corporate nature of the opinion is emphasized, and the first-person singular is not used (although the TV commentator, kin to the columnist, may say "I" if he pleases, and often does).

These two conventions, the editorial we and the faceless case maker, may be supported by reasoning that appears sound to the ownership of the publication or the broadcast channel. But they do lead to some awkward, even ludicrous excesses, particularly that pesky we. Here, for example, are some that got into print in professional, not student, publications:

- "As a matter of fact, we are a nonsmoker and have absolutely no use for cigarettes."
- "We attended a school district budget meeting the other night and came away shaking our head."
- "We are a former army propaganda officer, and so have a right to be suspicious."

The we convention can introduce confusion as well as awkwardness into editorial style. Sometimes a writer will want to use "we" to mean "we Americans," or "we New Yorkers," or "we, the people," yet in the next sentence he may use it as the editorial we, meaning the publication's faceless policy setters. Ambiguity and confusion abound.

If the convention is to be continued it would seem preferable to use some such expression as "this newspaper" or "this magazine" whenever the editorial we is meant.

There are, however, those who challenge the whole convention of corporate facelessness and who believe that editorials would be far more meaningful if they were signed individually and used the straightforward "I."

One editorial writer, Stephen Palmer of the *Lexington* (Ky.) *Leader,* observed:

> If we were really honest with ourselves we would freely admit that we like the myths which make our editorial words appear more than what they are—the writings of an individual, of several individuals, or a consensus opinion. We like the magic of myths; they help hide our shortcomings and make it more difficult for outsiders to fix the blame.
>
> . . . Some editorial writers actually hide behind the corporate image of the paper, particularly when they are asked to write the views of the editor or the publisher, which may or may not be their own. To those who feel that they are merely "hired guns" for management, unsigned editorials solve a problem both for the writer and the publisher who is unwilling to have his name linked with a particular point of view which may be unpopular or controversial.
>
> Signed editorials, on the other hand, require the greatest amount of honesty, personal integrity, and willingness to give the other side a chance to know its accusers. Most of us are not willing to be that honest, that courageous, or that open in today's society.[5]

One publication that did decide to venture out from behind the faceless convention is the *National Observer,* a weekly newsmagazine in newspaper format. The publication's editors and directors decided not only to do away with the editorial we and the unsigned editorial, but to make an even more dramatic break with tradition. They replaced the conventional editorial column with a new feature under the standing headline, "Observations." The contributions presented under this head are no longer the product of an editorial board, but of individual staff members—any staff members who might have something pertinent and thoughtful to say, not just the regular editorial writers. In explaining the change-over in a signed editorial statement, *Observer* editor Henry Gemmill wrote:

> For reasons obscured in the mists of the history of early print shops, it has become established custom for newspapers— including this one, up to now—to publish editorials. Unsigned, an editorial presumably proclaims the opinion of the newspaper.
>
> Because of advances in popular sex education, it would be hard nowadays to find even a very young child who believes the myth that babies are delivered by storks. Storks are birds. *People* make babies.

Despite a lag in popular journalism education, probably not too many children—or even adults—really believe the myth that newspapers have opinions. Newspapers are products. *People* make opinions.

So you could say we're just getting around to acknowledging the facts of life.[6]

While not going so far as the *Observer,* some other publications have made some gestures toward getting away from the faceless, corporate convention. Editorial writers from the *Louisville Courier-Journal,* the *Portland Oregonian,* and a number of other papers emerge once a week from behind the masthead to write signed columns (some with inset pictures of the writers) of personal opinion, reminiscence, or what have you. They still, however, write most of their work as unsigned contributions to the regular editorial section on the left-hand side of the page.

NO MORE THE BAD FATHER?

If the trend toward personalization were to continue it might serve to offset what one California newspaperman, Dan Anderson, has identified as an unfortunate characteristic of editorial style.

Anderson points out that psychiatry has revealed that the child tends to view his father as two individuals—the "good father" who offers love and gifts and the "bad father" who on occasion is the stern disciplinarian. And, Anderson suggests, many readers of opinion writing in magazines and newspapers may only too easily envision the authors as carryover manifestations of the bad-father image.

What is the nature of the "bad father"? He judges, chides, and chastises. He is inflexible, cold and remote. He imposes exhorbitant requirements. He knows everything and is inexorably, always right. The "bad father" is hard to talk back to . . . balks attempts to achieve independence, including independence of judgment. He stands for denial, restraint, restriction, embodying authority. He is excessively formal.[7]

And, says Anderson, the shoe fits the typical editorial writer as the reader pictures him. To do away with the unfortunate association, he suggests that opinion writers cultivate a more informal, casual style, drop the lecturer approach, and above all, *sign their pieces.*

Some of the informality and casualness that Anderson recommends has come into editorial writing in recent years. But except for the case of the *National Observer* and a handful of other publications, the convention of the unsigned editorial continues to hold sway and probably will for some time to come.

Let's turn now from consideration of editorial writing style to examine some specific writing problems, particularly those involved with getting into and getting out of an opinion piece.

THOSE VITAL FIRST MOMENTS

As the opinion writer settles down to his typewriter, his line of argument well-checked and polished until it is brilliant and flawless, he is approaching a make-or-break point in the overall effort to bring about a successful communication between him and his audience.

The editorialist's colleague on the news side, the reporter, knows the pivotal role that the lead plays in the effectiveness of the news story; if he fails to bring off the lead, the rest of the story may well be wasted. With the lead he snares the attention of the reader and hopes to hold it long enough so that he can get the rest of his message across.

To the opinion writer the lead is, if anything, even more important than it is to the news reporter.

In the case of the reporter, there is usually some built-in reader interest he can count on to draw an audience; at least some of his potential readers are going to be intrigued by the news topic he is reporting. This is less the case with the editorial writer, since he is offering opinion or explanation rather than fresh and sensational tidings.

Moreover, the editorialist is in some respects swimming upstream; he is trying to persuade—make a case—and he must expect that a good many of those in his audience are likely to be resistant, if not downright hostile, to the point of view he is advancing.

So, for the editorial writer, the lead must be as effective as he can possibly make it. And he labors under a bothersome but necessary technical handicap in trying to make it effective. For, unlike the news story lead, the editorial lead cannot blurt out all the exciting details in the first summary sentence. Typically, the editorial lead attempts to identify the topic but does *not* give away all of the case that the body of the piece will attempt to make. The editorial writer has to practice the art of suspended interest that the feature writer or the striptease dancer uses, gradually unveiling the full splendor of what he has to offer as the editorial develops.

If he gives everything away at the start—as the spot news story lead typically does—the editorial writer may lose his audience at that point. The reader may have little incentive to plow on through the evidence or the argumentation.

So most opinion writers try to follow two general principles in fashioning leads. They try to make clear what topic they are going to discuss, and they also try to offer some indication of the position that they will be outlining. The latter is a matter of fairness to the reader or auditor; he should be put on notice so that he can evaluate the arguments as they are laid out.

In most cases, these two elements, the topic identification and a clue to the position to be taken, are worked into the language of the lead. But some newspaper and magazine editorialists have taken an even more explicit approach—they set out a summing-up sentence in italics or boldface type at the very beginning as a sort of distillation of the central argument. Here's an example from the *Seattle Post-Intelligencer:*

An Ominous Statute

A P-I View: Congress should repeal Title II of the 1950 Internal Security Act. Congress has an opportunity to erase one of the great blots in American history. The chance will come in early September when the U.S. House of Representatives will vote. . . .

And then the editorial continued with its discussion of the case against Title II.

The *Los Angeles Times* experimented for a while with a similar introductory summary sentence, but later abandoned it. There is some disadvantage in using the device because it requires boiling down the editorial theme to what amounts to headline language. In the process there will almost inevitably be some oversimplification, perhaps even distortion. Then the reader will embark on the editorial with what may be a misconception.

Some editors have experimented successfully with a precede element that is not a conclusion but simply a statement of the issue to be explored in the body of the editorial. This identifies the agenda but avoids forcing a point of view on the reader before the justifying argument has been developed.

PLANTING THE HOOK

In devising a lead that will introduce the topic and give some clue to the stand to be advanced, the opinion writer must constantly bear in mind another function of those crucial opening lines. He must somehow arrest the reader's or listener's attention, just as the trout fly attracts the fish's eye. Then he must set the hook so that he can keep his audience on the line. And, to prolong the simile, the editorialist must in effect try to do this job with a barbless hook, because the reader or listener—unlike the hapless trout—can wriggle off effortlessly any time he loses interest.

Writing a lead that will accomplish these several objectives is never easy. An editorial writer may make a dozen tries before he is satisfied that he has done the best he can with the material at hand. But the effort is necessary. If the lead never does take shape the writer might as well stop right there, since the chances of salvaging the rest of the piece are slender.

Perhaps the commonest form of editorial lead is one based on a *news peg*. The writer attempts to capitalize on the reader's interest in and familiarity with something very recently in the news. Here is one example:

> The fatal mauling of a tourist by one of the Yellowstone Park bears earlier this week put the National Park Service under increased pressure to improve its safety programs.

If the news peg involved is strong enough, the writer can make good use of it to get the editorial under way and to intrigue the reader sufficiently to keep him moving on into the editorial.

But there is a built-in hazard with the news peg lead. When the writer tries to weld together the news angle, the topic identification, and the clue to the position he is going to develop, he may wind up with an unwieldy combination. Consider this one:

> The defection of Senator Hugh Scott of Pennsylvania from the ranks of those opposing legislative restrictions on the war-making powers of the presidency may serve to bring about a wide public discussion of the issue and eventual enactment of legislation, developments to be welcomed.

The writer has wedged in all the requisite elements, but he has also constructed so complex and cumbersome a lead that many readers may never get any farther.

There is another problem inherent in use of the news peg lead—its presumption that the reader is sufficiently familiar with the news event involved so that he can readily grasp the reference. To be sure, the opinion writer has as his target the thoughtful reader who does attend to the news, but even the opinion leaders, the influentials, do not comb through every item in the newspaper. And the editorialist, a deeply informed specialist in his subject, may not always be a good judge of how much the reader can be expected to hold in memory. The maxim, never *underestimate* the intelligence or *overestimate* the knowledge of your audience, is one for the opinion writer to memorize.

MAKING PICTURES

Another lead device that has utility for the opinion writer is that of *imagery*. The use of simile or metaphor as a means of getting into an editorial lead can be doubly helpful. It provides a word picture, a striking or amusing allusion to catch the reader's attention; and it also can help to economize on precious editorial space.

More information can sometimes be conveyed by the skillful use of imagery than by an equivalent volume of straight exposition. Consider this example:

> The Senate Finance Committee's hearings on the Administration tax bill is a little like what the three blind men said about the elephant. Each felt a different part of the creature's anatomy and they came to very different conclusions about what he must look like to people with sight. Recent witnesses before the committee have discussed differing aspects of the bill, and their testimony is notably divergent.

Consider how much wordier—and how much less interesting—this same lead might have been without the simile. (And note, too, that the writer filled in enough detail about the fable so that the reader would not miss the allusion; he did not make the mistake of assuming too much knowledge on the part of his audience.)

The use of imagery is particularly helpful to the editorialist if he is writing about a topic in which his readers will probably have scant interest (such as the tax bill in the example above). Many of the topics opinion writers must take up are in the low-interest category so far as most readers are concerned, and any device that makes them take on meaning and life aids the editorialist's chances of getting his theme across.

Here's another example of the adroit use of imagery in a piece about a subject few readers would be likely to find enthralling:

> It may turn out that the Treasury will be able to squeak through the next several months without bumping into the fed-

eral debt ceiling. But the spectacle of the government of the United States scraping pennies out of teapots and piggy banks in order to make ends meet legally is as ridiculous as it is unnecessary.

As with the news peg lead, however, there are some booby traps with the lead that is built around imagery. The figure of speech must be effectively devised, it must fit the situation, and it must be used with moderation—like garlic in cooking.

Look at some examples of violations of each of these basic rules. All of them appeared in major newspapers (the identities of which the author has mercifully masked by slight paraphrasing).

First, the metaphor that is wrong for the situation:

> The cracks appearing in the nuclear-power picture window are mostly in the ground where earth faults near reactors have raised fears of heavy radioactive contamination of the environment in case of major quakes.

Second, the metaphor that is just plain inept, badly devised:

> The provincial boundaries of academic freedom are riding in a static boat that is being steadily rocked by students all over the country.

And, finally, the garlic fault. This excerpt comes from the second and third paragraphs of an editorial dealing with a congressional investigation into alleged infiltration of our government:

> In this age when subversion is an acknowledged arm of Soviet diplomacy, it is inevitable and proper that Congress should look into the barrel of United States bureaucracy to see that no rotten apples are there.
>
> But the current congressional probers, in their wide-ranging hunt for political carrion, frequently are shooting dangerously wide of the mark.

Had the writer stopped with the rotten apple bit he might have been all right; it's corny, but it serves. Instead he suddenly shifts us off on a hunting expedition for carrion (which seems a bit pointless, since carrion is by definition already dead) and then warns about missing the mark (and hitting the wrong carrion, perhaps?). Whether all of this has been going on in the apple barrel where we began is never quite clear.

Imagery has many virtues in opinion writing, as it does in fiction writing. But it must be handled with a sure and imaginative touch. It can go so wrong, so easily. Yet when it is good it is very, very good. ("From the head of the West German Republic, perched almost within the jaws of Soviet power, has come a message of high hope and brisk optimism.")

QUESTIONS AND QUOTES

When a visual device will not fit the situation, a *question lead* may do an effective job of launching the editorial and also of engaging the attention of the audience. The question lead, in effect, opens a conversation directly with the reader, drawing him in.

> How long will Ted Kennedy have to wait before the memory of that tragic night on Chappaquiddick Island fades from the minds of the American voters?

If the question is carefully phrased it can indicate the topic and the stand of the editorial just as clearly as any other approach could:

> Will the voters of the country express a clear choice for president at the polls next year only to find their intent frustrated through vengeful dog-in-the-manger tactics in the South?

But of course it must be a legitimate question, one that fits the situation and isn't trumped-up as a gimmick to get the reader's attention. The phony question is as much to be avoided as overripe imagery.

Similar caution ought to be used with *quote leads*. If the quote is a pertinent one, and if its source can be indicated quickly so the reader is not long left in the dark, it can be an effective beginning:

> Said San Francisco Police Chief Thomas Cahill, after the ugly New Year's eve rioting in his city, "The trend of the times is outright defiance of authority."

But if the quote is a lengthy one, and the identification of the speaker is delayed, the result may be unfortunate:

> "Whether we locate the auditorium in the center of downtown or out on the fringes of the city depends upon the degree to which the expected traffic congestion could be handled, not in any sense on the question of financing." This was the view of

Alderman Claude Stines, as expressed at yesterday's meeting of the City Council.

If the reader is obliged to go back over the quote a second time to reevaluate it after he has been told who is speaking, he may not be willing to take the trouble; he will very likely shift off to some other item that doesn't make him work so hard.

And if the purported quote is patently improbable, the reader will turn away in disgust—or else clip the offending item to send in to the *New Yorker* magazine's "Quotes We Doubt Ever Were . . ." department.

ONCE UPON A TIME . . .

Some editorials or opinion essays can be opened on an anecdotal note, if there is space to work with. This tack is really better suited to the magazine writer or the columnist than it is to the newspaper editorialist, who usually has to operate within tight space limits.

This was the lead on an opinion piece that eventually got around to discussing the preservation of a mountain valley:

> Kneeling at the edge of the craggy New England seacoast, the scientist carefully examines a heron's egg. The egg, and 12 others like it nestled among the nearby rocks, are unknowingly part of an important experiment. Scientists are attempting to learn exactly what variables result in some eggs of this diminishing species hatching healthy young, while doomed weaker shells crack prematurely.
>
> Hours after the scientist concludes his daily observations, a group of men scramble along the shore, passing over the nesting area. Some of the eggs are crushed; the experiment is ruined.

The writer finally worked in a parallel with the mountain valley he was concerned about, but he used up great gobs of precious space in the process. Most of the time, the newspaper editorialist could not allow himself that luxury.

But he can use a variation of the anecdotal lead, one citing a series of illustrative cases, as does the following editorial page item from the *Minneapolis Tribune:*

> A Minneapolis company sends an executive to meet with the management of its Tokyo affiliate. A market analyst for a St. Paul manufacturer visits several Latin American cities. A Twin Cities family departs for a holiday in Europe. These common-

place occurences, together with the continued growth of air travel between this metropolitan area and others in the United States, present both a problem and an opportunity for the Twin Cities.

Whatever lead device he chooses (and the above is, of course, by no means an exhaustive catalog of the possibilities), the opinion writer shapes it with as much care and precision as he can muster. He knows that this is a key moment in his temporary relationship with the reader or viewer and that, if he cannot make effective contact at this stage, the effort that has gone into building the main body of argumentation will have been wasted.

CURTAIN LINES

Another key moment comes at the close of the editorial or column, after the lines of argument have been laid down and the persuasive case fitted together, piece by piece. Perhaps the most pertinent counsel to be offered the would-be opinion writer at this stage is to practice restraint. Once the argumentation has been completed, the final nail driven home, there is a natural note of climax, and most editorials probably could and should end right there. (One experienced editor once advised the author that "the only right way to end an editorial is with a period.")

But the temptation is great to keep on writing or talking, to add an extra flourish, one more burst of rhetoric. The temptation ought to be avoided, since the effect of the added-on bit is usually unfortunate. It is likely either to represent overkill (". . . nauseated by the stink of an awful halitosis of the political soul") or to convey an impression of repetitiveness.

Instead of tacking something on to the end of his completed case, the opinion writer is better advised to plan the *line of argument* so that its ending note is a memorable one—and then let the editorial or the column end there, too. The findings of communication research suggest that the arguments presented at the beginning or at the end of a communication are likely to be better remembered than some of those embedded in the body of the message.[8] So these last moments with the reader ought to be meaningful and telling ones; an editorial that overreaches at the end or else trails off lamely may well fail in its purpose even if it has been well constructed in the earlier stages.

Perhaps the most effective form of finish for the opinion piece is a restatement of the main thrust of the argument, but with a fresh orientation. If this restatement can involve some word picture, some device of imagery, all the better.

One editorial critical of a bureaucrat who had been meddling with the Bureau of Standards and trying to introduce pressure politics into the workings of that agency, closed with the following:

> The politically inspired intervention of Mr. Weeks had the effect of casting under suspicion the integrity of an agency that is supposed to be the very standard of reliability for the nation. Any outcome of the dispute that left lingering doubts would have been unsatisfactory. As it is, there are no loose ends left dangling —they are all wrapped around Mr. Weeks's neck.

The reader left that article with a vivid memory that contained, built into it, the theme of the editorial argument.

Such finishing gambits as "The time for action is now!," "We have every confidence in the good sense of the American people," "Let every parent search his conscience," and "The nation will be watching" fall into the category of editorialese and contribute very little to the strength of an editorial in its important closing moments.

WHAT GOES BETWEEN

The body of the editorial is of course the case making, which has already been explored at some length earlier in this book. But there are some tactical or structural points to be noted about the main body of the editorial that are not related to argumentation.

What, for example, about the matter of length? How long should an opinion piece be?

Obviously, space and time considerations differ from medium to medium. Space is limited on the newspaper editorial page, and time on the air is equally tight. A magazine editorial can be more exhaustive, and the opinion journals can, if they wish, devote whole articles—or even whole issues—to a single major topic.

Many newspaper editors and broadcast managers insist that opinion pieces be kept brief, and they argue that this is not only to save space or time. They believe firmly that an editorial expression will not get any attention from the reader if it is lengthy (one newspaper has a standing rule that no editorial can be longer than the number of words that can be typed, double-spaced, on a half sheet of standard 8-1/2-by-11-inch typing paper).

But this insistence on brevity is challenged by some other editors and some scholars in the field of communication research. Dr. Chilton R. Bush, for many years head of the Department of Communication at Stanford University, once observed:

> The editorial writer who discusses an important, complex problem can't risk trying to influence such readers [the best informed and thoughtful readers] about something important in a 300 to 400 word space. If he fails to cover all of the bases, some smart guy in the group (who happens to disagree with his objectives) will point this out to the others. The editorial, therefore, should use as much space as is required for organizing and presenting all the arguments.[9]

And the editor of a distinguished small-city newspaper's editorial page, William F. Johnston of the *Lewiston* (Idaho) *Tribune,* expressed a similar viewpoint:

> Some years ago, I was squirming through a rough session at an American Press Institute at Columbia University. The editorial page editor of a metropolitan daily, who had done a lot of advance work to help us with our problems, was tearing apart the editorials of our individual newspapers. He was especially outspoken when he got around to mine.
>
> "Your editorials are too long," he said. "Also, they are too complex and too intellectual. If you want to attract readership, you have to stick to simple topics, use short, punchy sentences, and deal in personalities now and then. Aim for the average reader. He isn't interested in abstractions. Keep your stuff punchy."
>
> I ventured to disagree in theory, although I confess I must concede some points in fact. Most of my editorials *are* too long. I never seem to have enough time to write a short one.
>
> Nevertheless, the emphasis upon audience size which may be very proper on the comics page, or on the television screen, must be deflated considerably, it seems to me, before it is applied to the editorial page.
>
> An editorial should make a complex issue as understandable as possible through the use of clear logic and simple language. But important issues cannot be ignored simply because they may be complex. And abstract arguments usually cannot be reduced to personalities without destroying editorial integrity.
>
> If some readers—perhaps a swiftly growing number of readers—

are too lazy, too ignorant, or too indifferent to bother reading editorials devoid of personal pronouns, catch phrases, and allusions to sex, that is not necessarily the fault of the editorial writer. Perhaps such readers would be happier perusing the comic books or absorbing the soap operas in any case. The editorial writer, at least, will not be able to help them much by depriving more curious and more literate readers of ideas that may be worth expressing even if they cannot capture the mass market.[10]

An opinion piece ought to be long enough to cover the topic, do the job it sets out to do. Brevity is indeed a virtue, and a vast expanse of gray type—or a lengthy essay on the air—may indeed be too forbidding to hold the attention of some readers or listeners. But the thesis advanced by Bush and Johnston is persuasive, and it makes sounder sense than the philosophy expressed in the half-page limit earlier cited.

THE STRAIGHT, STRONG LINE

One other general point should be made about the opinion piece as a whole. Textbooks in news writing use the inverted-pyramid diagram to suggest the form of the spot news story, with the main elements at the beginning and other items arranged in order of descending importance as the story continues.

The feature story frequently tends to be structured toward a climactic ending, an O. Henry kicker that surprises, delights, or shocks the reader.

The editorial, however, can perhaps best be represented diagrammatically as a straight, strong line. The opinion piece is most effective if the central theme, the core, is always in view. The transitions should be tight-fitting; there should be no digressions, no diversionary excursions.

The piece may use suspended interest to some degree; it may build to a climax. But it must always possess a sense of unity, it must strike a strong, memorable note. The editorial that tries to juggle several themes simultaneously is not likely to be successful with any of them.

NOTES

1. Henry Fairlie, "Anglo-American Differences," *Encounter,* June 1966, pp. 73–86.

2. *Ibid.,* p. 84.

3. Creed C. Black, "Middle Ground Breeds Vapidity," *Bulletin of the American Society of Newspaper Editors,* October 1, 1966, p. 5.

4. "The Case of the Obscene Cash Register," lead editorial in *San Francisco Chronicle,* December 10, 1970.

5. Stephen Palmer, "Editorials and Myth-Making," *Masthead,* Spring 1971, pp. 21-22.

6. Henry Gemmill, quoted from the March 8, 1971 issue of *National Observer,* in *Masthead,* Summer 1971, p. 42.

7. Dan Anderson, "Got That Unread Feeling? See a Psychiatrist!" *American Editor,* October 1959, pp. 28-35.

8. A study that produced this finding is reported in Marvin Karlins and Herbert I. Abelson, *Persuasion,* New York, Springer Publishing Co., 1970, pp. 30-32.

9. Chilton R. Bush, "Two Basic Misapprehensions About Editorials," *Bulletin of the American Society of Newspaper Editors,* August 1, 1958, p. 12.

10. William F. Johnston, managing editor of the *Lewiston* (Idaho) *Tribune,* in a speech to the Rocky Mountain Collegiate Press Association at Pocatello, Idaho, on April 10, 1959.

10
Variations on the Theme

"The ways of love are infinitely varied," according to a romantic (and evidently ingenious) poet. Something nearly so sweeping could be said about the ways of writing. And even journalistic writing—including editorial writing—is susceptible to flexible and imaginative treatment, despite the guidelines and frameworks that have been discussed in earlier chapters of this book.

An expression of opinion may be conveyed to the audience by means of many different kinds of literary vehicles, even if the variety may not be quite so extensive as the lover's.

It is certainly true that *most* of the editorial expressions one encounters in the mass media of communication are cast in the form of conventional argumentation and exposition; this approach best suits both the purposes and the deadlines of the editorialist. But the opinion writer is typically a versatile practitioner when he has a little room to maneuver, not a "Johnny-One-Note" wedded to a single approach. And there are topics and occasions that lend themselves to variations on the conventional pattern. In this chapter we'll look over an illustrative sampler (not meant to be a comprehensive catalog) of such variations and note some of their strengths and their weaknesses.

(The editorial cartoon is of course one of these variant approaches, but it is so highly developed and specialized an editorial vehicle that it deserves separate treatment in a later chapter.)

SOMETIMES THE PICADOR

From time to time the opinion writer will find it possible to make an editorial point simply by underlining something in the news that the reader might otherwise have failed to note. Allan Nevin's excellent compilation of editorial quotations from colonial times to the present, *American Press Opinion, Washington to Coolidge,* cites an early example of this approach.[1]

Shortly before the turn of the century, Nevins relates, a Philadelphia newspaper reprinted on its editorial page, without any additional comment, two news stories that had appeared in its previous day's issue. One of the stories dealt with the efforts of the management of the Wanamaker department store to resist an employee request for a few more cents an hour in wages. The other story recounted, under a Paris dateline, the details of a $20,000 dinner party given by a Wanamaker son on holiday abroad. The stories were positioned side by side, and there was no necessity for explaining the editorial point.

A more recent example involved a single news story. The editorialist spotted the following UPI lead in the day's news budget:

> **CANNES (UPI)**—The U.S. Navy invited Zsa Zsa Gabor and a flock of movie stars aboard the aircraft carrier "Intrepid" today for a cocktail party but barred reporters on grounds of "military secrets."

The editorial writer simply ran the lead as is in his editorial column, under the headline "No Comment." None was necessary.

This kind of editorial device is a form of pin sticking. It does not allow for a careful, balanced examination of issues. But it serves effectively to plant a dart in the hide of a target, as a picador does in the bullring to wound rather than kill. It calls the reader's or viewer's attention to an aspect of a news event or a news personality that, in the opinion writer's judgment, warrants critical attention.

One college newspaper editor, combing through back files, one day found in a 1948 issue of his paper a full-page ad featuring a photograph of a movie actor plugging a cigarette brand. The actor was a very youthful Ronald Reagan, and he was quoted as saying, "My cigarette is the MILD cigarette . . . that's why Chesterfield is my favorite." He was identified as the star of "The Voice of the Turtle," a Warner Brothers production. The college editor reprinted the ad in slightly reduced format, but still occupying most of the editorial page, with the caption in large type at one side:

> The Honorable Ronald Reagan, Governor of the 31st state of the Union, California.

There was no other comment, and the reader was left to make of it what he would. This was a picador device, based in this instance on ridicule of the qualifications of the movie-star-turned-politician, and it could not be described as a balanced evaluation. But that was not what the editorialist intended in this instance.

Thrusts of this sort are one-dimensional in nature, and their legitimacy as editorial expressions depends to considerable degree on the complexity of the subject involved. The brief reference to the cocktail party aboard the *Intrepid* made a valid point, and made it well. Whether the reprinted ad featuring Governor Reagan could be as easily defended is open to question. What a man's occupation was 23 years ago may have nothing whatever to do with how effectively he is equipped to handle his present-day assignment. The borderline between valid editorial comment and simplistic name calling is sometimes faint.

ART AS EDITORIAL

The one-dimensional disadvantages of the pin-jab editorial also apply to some extent to the use of charts, graphs, or other kinds of art (using the term in the journalistic sense) as opinion vehicles.

The graph on page 114 was published on the editorial page, as a self-contained editorial without any additional text, in a college newspaper.[2] It juxtaposes a quotation from President Nixon at the time of the incursion of American forces into Cambodia in 1970 to the graph, which shows the rise in American combat deaths in the month that followed. The contrast is telling, and the overall impact of the pictorial editorial is strong.

Some readers of the newspaper objected vigorously to the use of the graph, contending that it grossly oversimplified a complex situation and arguing that the destruction of Viet Cong forces in Cambodia would result in the saving of many American lives in later stages of the Vietnam withdrawal. Others responded that the graph editorial was entirely defensible as it stood, even if it did constitute some oversimplification; the contrast between the chief executive's promise and the facts depicted by the rising line of combat deaths spoke for itself, no matter what other speculative or background factors might be taken into consideration. You are free to accept either line of argument. The point is, however, that such editorial expressions tend to be both hard-hitting and simplistic—for which reasons they are likely to provoke, and be vulnerable to, critical rejoinders.

Sometimes a more complicated use of art as editorial can offset to some extent the one-dimensional disadvantages.

One metropolitan paper, concerned about slum-housing conditions in its community, devoted its entire editorial page one day to a set of pictures taken by one of its photographers who had toured the ghetto area the previous afternoon. The pictures showed rotting garbage piled up in hallways, stopped-up plumbing fixtures black with grime and disuse, and even, in one horrifying shot, a large, plump rat crawling into a baby's crib. The impact of the page on the readers was undoubtedly far greater than would have been the case had the matter been treated in conventional editorial prose, however impassioned and graphic.

Yet there was no way to discuss, through the picture display, some of the complexities underlying the grisly surface facts—the matter of re-

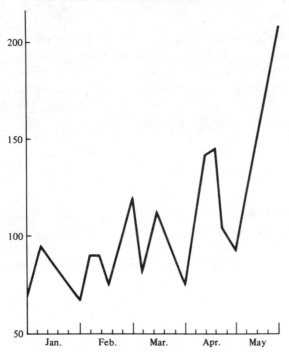

U.S. Combat Deaths in Indochina—1970

"A majority of the American people want to keep the casualties of our brave men in Vietnam at an absolute minimum. The action I take [in Cambodia] is essential if we are to accomplish that goal." President Nixon, April 30, [1970]

sponsibility (was it the fault of the slum-housing owners? of the tenants who had been misusing the properties? of the city's health and building inspectors who had been lax in their duties?) or the question of how conditions were going to be improved.

But these matters could be taken up in later, conventional editorials. There was no doubt about the value of the picture page as a means of arresting the reader's attention; it was then up to the editorial writers to follow up with the more detailed analyses and recommendations in subsequent issues.

Another paper, the *Providence Journal,* once used a pictorial editorial display to excellent effect in meeting a "duty editorial" obligation. This type of editorial is occasioned by holidays, anniversaries, and other recurrent events or problems that by custom call for editorial comment; it becomes a trying and wearisome task to think up new changes to ring on stale themes.

In this case the issue was traffic safety. Instead of a conventional "Drive safely, the life you save . . ." sort of editorial, the paper ran a full page made up of a montage of headlines of fatal-accident stories published in the paper during the previous year, arranged around a single picture of a particularly violent two-car collision. There was a small block of text, but the theme was carried by the headlines and their cumulative impact.[3]

QUIZ TIME

The value of questions as lead devices was noted earlier. But sometimes an entire editorial, not just the lead, can be structured around the question format.

In an editorial designed to explain the likely effect of a fair-housing bill then pending in Congress, the *St. Louis Post-Dispatch* once used a question–answer format throughout the piece. The writer posed hypothetical average-man questions in italics, responding to each concisely but comprehensively in regular type, then going on to the next question, and so on.

In a more elaborate variation on this approach, an editorial writer on another paper spent several days going from door to door in his metropolitan community questioning housewives and men in the street about the problem of inflation, then an urgent concern. From their responses, he identified a series of misconceptions that appeared to be widespread and then devoted several editorials to taking these up one by one, explaining in what respects each was ill-founded and what the realities of the problems were. It was an educative effort, based on identified existing knowledge gaps rather than on hypothetical ones.

Other opinion writers have experimented with a quiz approach, posing questions with multiple-response answers for the reader to pick from but providing the correct answers only at the end of the editorial, in the fashion of test-yourself features in magazines. This approach gets the reader involved, as have similarly structured broadcast presentations (e.g., on traffic safety), and this facilitates the persuasion process or the education process.

The editorialist has to have a sure touch in using such offbeat devices as the quiz-show format or the Q–A sequence. They can't be stretched out too far, nor can they be used too often. But if the writer does have a sensitive hand, he can make excellent use of them. The following, for example, is an editorial from the Eugene (Oreg.) *Register-Guard*. All of its points are made through the sequence of questions, and the writer knew just how far he could carry the device without the repetitive effect becoming irritating to the reader:

Some Questions

Why, why in the world, did upwards of 4,000 people, good citizens for the most part, cluster around Hayden Bridge over the weekend? What did they hope to see as they watched skin divers search for an automobile that had reportedly gone into the deepest part of the McKenzie River?

And Sunday morning, when the car was brought to the surface, why did they rush forward to see what was inside? What pleasure did they hope to get from seeing that a woman, dead, was inside the automobile? Did the sight give them the "kicks" they had come to get?

Were these people the people who are chronic spectators at all the big fires? Did they watch the search and recovery operation with the same "sidewalk superintendent" emotions that govern the frustrated fire chiefs who "direct" the fighting of a big fire? Deep down in their hearts did they hope the car would prove empty? Or would they have been disappointed if no body had been found?

Why did they ignore the pleas of authorities who asked them not to get in the way? As they look back on the events of the weekend, what satisfaction do they get?[4]

Another unusual—though quite different—use of the question approach was made by a writer who built the piece out of answers rather than questions. He wanted to comment on the inappropriateness of a judicial appointment just announced by the governor in his state. So he used as his editorial the results of a state bar association poll, in which all the lawyers in the state had been asked how potential candidates for the judgeship ranked in terms of their qualifications. It was a long list and it ranged in descending order of preference, with the leading candidate having 237 votes as best qualified and the last name on the list having 25. The writer then ended the editorial with the observation that the man whom the governor had just raised to the bench hadn't made the list at all—not even with a single vote. And he titled the editorial: "The Little Man Who Wasn't There."

HELP FROM THE ARTS

The forms of drama and verse sometimes tempt the opinion writer. Both have some advantages as vehicles for editorial themes, and both have disadvantages.

Structuring an opinion piece as a playlet, for example, may provide some dividends in reader interest. And sometimes additional dimensions of a situation can be conveyed more easily in the form of dialog than exposition. But setting the stage, erecting the scenery, and sketching in the backdrop may take up much valuable space and thereby offset the advantages to be gained from use of the format.

This doesn't have to be the case, of course. Consider this very brief but effective example:

Drama in Eugene

As the curtain opens, a teenage girl, shabbily dressed, is standing near a cash register. Behind the counter is a man clerk. Behind the girl and elsewhere nearby are assorted citizens of various ages, sexes and apparent degrees of affluence.

GIRL bends over counter and says something softly to CLERK.
CLERK booms out in loud voice: "Welfare? It doesn't say welfare. Where's your welfare slip?"
The curtain falls for all except those who witnessed it.[5]

No wasted words, and a point about insensitivity in human relations graphically made. But only that one point; the more complex the theme to be worked through, the more extensive the dramaturgic structure would have to be. And then concern about space might come into consideration.

Verse offers other kinds of pitfalls, if the editorial writer chooses that route. The writing of effective poetry calls for a special genius, and someone who may be deft enough at writing straight prose may become over-cute or all thumbs when he decides to take a stab at poetry.

If he is willing to borrow from a more practiced hand, he can use parody, fitting his theme onto the structure that another poet has already built. This usually turns out far more successfully than when the opinion writer attempts to start from scratch.

One editorial in the form of parody of a familiar poem was inspired by a particularly ludicrous bureaucratic stalemate involving two agencies of state government in Rhode Island. Along the shores of Narragansett Bay there are many inlets where a prized bivalve, the quahaug (it makes magnificent chowder) can be harvested by men who use long wooden rakes, or tongs, to comb through the mud bottoms below the shallow waters. There is a season during which such harvest is legal, but poaching out of season is commonplace. Two agencies of the state government, the Fish and Game Commission and the Harbors and Rivers Bureau, shared jurisdiction over the poaching problem; because of interagency rivalries, they were not cooperating efficiently. As the two agencies squabbled about whose responsibility it was to move in on the busy poachers, someone suggested that perhaps ships from the Newport Naval Base nearby might be used to cope with the situation. This was the last straw, and an editorial writer for the *Providence* (R.I.) *Journal* (not this author) chose to frame his comment on the situation in verse parody. If you have followed all the above background, you're ready for it:

The Looting of Allen Harbor
or, A Brief Lesson
in the Virtues
of Planned Government Liaison

A bunch of the boys were whooping it up in Allen Harbor Bay;
The kids that handle the quahaug tongs were making golden hay.
Sitting offshore in a fancy craft was a crew from Fish and Game.
But they wouldn't budge to spoil the fun 'til a Proper Order came.

"We've closed the bay by the law's advice," Harbors and Rivers
    said,
"But we're up the creek without a boat, and our faces are very
    red."
"That's very sad," replied Fish and Game, "but there's nothing
    we can do.
"Still the Navy's at hand with plenty of brass, and supercarriers,
    too."
But the captain he was busy, and couldn't be readily reached.
So the supercarriers stayed at dock and other craft stayed
    beached.
And the kids that handle the quahaug tongs continued to make
    their hay
'Til the craft were loaded gunwale-deep with shellfish from the
    bay.

"A pox on you all," said Harbors and Rivers, still stranded on the
    shore,
"We're killing the order to close the bay and we'll never come
    here any more."
So Fish and Game and admirals, too, stood by to watch the sport,
As tongers' skiffs swarmed into the harbor from every bayside
    port.

The air was fresh, the bay was calm, the quahaugs fat as money.
For the Navy and our own dear state, the snafu was a honey.
The moral's clear for all to read, the dopey and the clever—
That men may come and men may go, but red tape rules forever.

That may not be deathless verse, but it was effective satire in the
situation. Original poetry, without the assist from the professional poet
that the parodist uses, does not often turn out well in the editorial
columns, however. But that doesn't stop some opinion writers from
trying it.

FOURTH LEADERS

There is another kind of variation on the conventional theme that
involves not form so much as content. In Great Britain newspaper
editorials are called "leaders," and on some editorial pages there is a
strong tradition that each day the "fourth leader," the final editorial in
the section, must be a special kind of piece—one light in tone and
subject. Its purpose is to provide a change of diet from the heavier,

meat-and-potatoes fare that is set out in the earlier editorials in the section. While not so institutionalized, a similar tradition is observed on many American editorial pages. As often as possible, there is included in the editorial budget one piece, usually brief, that is lively and amusing in tone.

Some papers finesse the tradition by using a humorist-columnist such as Art Buchwald or Russell Baker. Other editorial page editors seek to offer a sort of counterfeit fourth leader by working up pieces of sugary rhapsody about nature or the change of seasons. A true change-of-pace editorial, however, has three characteristics:

It is light and deft in tone, and it somehow tickles the reader's funnybone.

It is pegged in some fashion on the current news.

And it has a legitimate editorial point to make, if only briefly—the illumination of some absurd facet of human behavior, the pinpointing of an illogical inconsistency, or the exposure of some malfeasance or nonfeasance by someone who ought to know better.

The third ingredient is difficult to build into the light editorial, and a great many opinion writers find this kind of piece the most difficult of all to write.

The writer may sense the germ of such a piece in a news item in the morning's paper, but then struggle in vain to bring off just the right combination of humor, pinprick, and wry anatomizing of some semiserious issue that the situation requires.

Consider an actual example. A brief news item appeared in the morning paper, reporting that a man named Mayo had been saving string for eight years, wrapping each salvaged piece into a gradually expanding ball. The ball now weighed 2,400 pounds and was estimated to contain 3,260,000 feet of string. End of news item.

The editorial writer noted the piece and decided there ought to be the basis for a lively little light editorial in it. He wrote the piece, largely consisting of a rehearsal of the facts in the news story and a contrast between the string saver's situation and that in the writer's household, where no one could ever find any string when it was needed. And he wound up the piece:

> Yet we do not foresee the day we might need 3,260,000 feet of string. Mr. Mayo, on the other hand, does not foresee the day he might not need that much. We and Mr. Mayo are ships that pass in the night, it seems, ships that pass in the night.

Although it was published as such, that really wasn't a legitimate light editorial. It was simply a repackaging of a news item, with a rather lame little addendum that did not justify the investment of space—and the writer's time.

What, instead, might have made a true three-dimensional light editorial of it? For one thing, the writer might have used the string saver and his enormous hoard as the springboard for a brief treatment of the spirit of acquisition buried within all of us and pressing to find an outlet in some fashion, sometimes without regard for the utility or worth of the material being acquired. That would have given the amusing oddity aspect of the piece some additional depth.

Take another case. A student editorial writer noted in the news an item from Detroit to the effect that a University of Illinois professor believed that the dramatic names being given to new auto models inspired their drivers to behave recklessly. He suggested using some less ·inflammatory tags. The editorial writer worked on the item for a time and came up with this:

> News from Detroit indicates that a University of Illinois professor is concerned about the racy names of America's newer, sportier cars—suggesting that he believes automobile appellations connoting horses and tigers and big birds are conducive to careless driving resulting in increased highway fatalities.
>
> A study will be made, the wire story assures us.
>
> Yet we doubt that, say, a renamed Mustang (a Mare?) or a new chrome label on the Firebird (the Pontiac Dove?) would have any effect other than to reduce auto sales.

He sensed that the piece hadn't worked out very well and took it to a more experienced colleague for suggestions. The colleague pointed out some cumbersome and pretentious wording ("automobile appellations connoting horses and tigers") that was out of place in a light piece. He also observed that the editorial didn't add much of anything to the material contained in the news item. Why not pick up the professor's concern about the effect of the names on the actions of the drivers and do something with that?

So the original writer ran it through his typewriter again, trying to build in a bit more substance, another plane. The result, which was then worth publishing:

> A University of Illinois professor is concerned about the racy

names of America's newer, sportier cars. He says that automobiles named after horses, tigers, and big birds give drivers dangerous delusions and lead to careless driving and increased highway fatalities.

A study will be made, the wire story reports.

The professor's theory may or may not be right. We're inclined to be skeptical. But in any case we think he ought to mind his own business and let the car names alone.

After all, there aren't many chances left in this depersonalized, automated, bomb-haunted world of ours for a fellow to assert himself as an individual. If he gets some ego-inflation from riding a proxy mustang, or tempest, or firebird, so what? It's a healthier outlet than wife-beating.

The light piece need not make a major editorial point—but it should contain the opinion dimension in some fashion. It can't get by only as a chuckle-rouser (there are dime-a-dozen syndicated fillers for that purpose).

A writer who can handle the light, change-of-pace editorial is a valued member of the staff, and rightly so. When such a piece is well done it can be something of a miniature masterpiece, and it can cover a surprising amount of territory.

Consider the following brief piece, first published on the editorial page of the *Providence Bulletin*. It takes aim at three different targets, and with gentle, deliberate understatement hits all of them squarely in a few more than 200 words. Note the skillful use of style, internal rhymes, and the pacing of sentence length to achieve the effect of conversation:

Rabbits—and the Tongue-Tied Marquess

The other day in Britain's House of Lords there was excitement, there was stir, there was a rustle as of a wind riffling the pages of *Burke's Peerage*. And there was reason.

George Horatio Charles, Fifth Marquess of Cholmondeley (pronounced Chumley) took his seat in Parliament in 1923. For 32 years his record for inactivity was unblemished, his silence unbroken. Rarely had he sat among the Peers, never had he spoken. Steadfast had he been in adherence to the principle laid down by Gilbert and Sullivan in *Iolanthe:* that Britain would be safe as long as members of the House of Lords "did nothing in particular and did it very well." Now, at 72, the Marquess was at long last on his feet, and duke nudged duke as over the benches the whisper ran, "Chumley is up."

What compulsion, what crisis of affairs, lifted the Marquess from his 32-year squat? Rabbits. They must, he said, be destroyed. Some years ago a rabbit disease was introduced into Britain to rid the realm of rabbits. It had not done so. Rabbits still infested dell and dingle, mated in pairs. Certain men of title had been lax in restricting rabbits to their own property. Drastic legislation was called for, stern pains and penalties, perhaps prison sentences. "If some noble lords meet in jail," declared the risen Chumley, "it will be their own fault." He then sat down, left the Peers to ponder his words. There'll always be an England. Also, one hopes, a Chumley. Possibly, too, a rabbit. The disease which was supposed to exterminate them, but didn't, is called myxomatosis, pronounced myxis.

NOTES

1. Allan Nevins, *American Press Opinion, Washington to Coolidge,* Boston, Heath, 1928.

2. *Oregon Daily Emerald,* University of Oregon, May 26, 1970, p. 6.

3. *Providence Journal,* January 7, 1957, p. 12.

4. The author sees this newspaper regularly and has over a number of years. It happens to have a particularly excellent editorial page, which accounts for the frequency with which examples from its columns are cited in this book. It's handy, true, but it's also very good, so no apologies are offered for drawing on it extensively.

5. From (surprise!) the *Eugene* (Oreg.) *Register-Guard.*

11
Old Wine in New Bottles

In journalism's early days the pamphleteers alone wielded the opinion function, insofar as the limited freedom of their era permitted. Later the newspapers and magazines enjoyed a long period during which they were the chief purveyors of prophecies and judgments. But today expressions of opinion flow to the public through many channels and in a variety of forms, as we noted at the beginning of this book.

There are editorial writers in the classic sense, there are columnists, magazine essayists, interpretive journalists, broadcast editorialists, and "new" journalists—each in his way attempting to give the public light and direction on its turbulent passage through a murky and perplexing world.

But whatever the channel and whatever the orientation, all of these various opinion peddlers use similar techniques. At the heart of their messages are the kinds of case making we have been exploring at length in this book. All of the nearly and distantly related kin of the editorial writer—whether columnist, TV commentator, or "new" journalist—muster evidence, summon witnesses, and bring into play the kinds of attention getting and argument building discussed in earlier chapters.

In other words, although the packaging varies, the principles and tactics of opinion writing we have been examining apply to *all* of the various forms that the opinion function takes in the mass media today.

Nevertheless, there is some point in taking a look at these various forms separately, if briefly. The reader should be aware of their distinctive characteristics, their individual ground rules, and the differences among them—partly as necessary background knowledge for anyone who would be an opinion writer and partly to be informed about the career options that these various channels afford. To provide such background information will be the purpose of this chapter.

SOBER VOICES AND RAUCOUS ONES

Let's look first at the *opinion journals,* both above and below ground. The writers for publications in this category are the present-day incarnation of the original pamphleteers in that the vehicles in which their work appears are devoted *chiefly* (in some cases entirely) to opinion; in most of the other mass media of communication, opinion is only one of many ingredients in the mixture of features they offer.

The opinion journals include long-established publications noted for their thoughtful if pointed case making (*Nation, National Review, Commentary,* and others) and also relative newcomers to the journalistic scene such as the underground and counterculture press (the Berkeley *Barb,* the Los Angeles *Oracle,* and many others) that often traffic in wild-swinging polemic.

At the soberer end of that wide spectrum, magazines such as the *New Republic* or *National Review* attract excellent and widely known contributors despite their modest circulations. (The permanent staff on such magazines may be small, however.) Whether as occasional contributor or permanent editor, those who write for the established opinion journals value the platform. It affords them a chance to deal at length with complex issues, without as much concern for the space or time strictures that limit the scope of the opinion function in the general circulation media.

The tone is typically serious (although William Buckley's *National Review* has flip and lively moments), and the articles constitute a blend of argumentation and evidence. Sometimes they also include news, in the form of exposés of matters not covered by the daily press. But the preoccupation is with the expression of opinion for an informed and thoughtful audience, if a small one (some sample circulations: *Nation,* 37,000; *New Republic,* 150,000; *National Review,* 100,000).

The underground and counterculture publications are more numerous than the established opinion journals, also more raucous and less responsible. An authority on magazine journalism, Roy Paul Nelson, estimates that there are several hundred such publications in the United States now, although the number fluctuates as arrivals and departures take place. He observes:

> The phenomenon of publications existing for the sole purpose of chipping away at established institutions is nothing new in America, of course; but the proliferation of them, the tone of their diatribes—that *is* new.

What makes them possible is the sullen mood of a by now rather sizable body of activists and revolutionaries, the permissiveness of the courts, and the availability of an inexpensive printing process, cheap, cold-type composition. Anyone with a commitment to the cause and a few dollars collected from sympathizers can enter the field.[1]

Those entrants have included such forerunners as the *Village Voice,* a Greenwich Village weekly paper founded in 1955 (and now looked upon by the *nouveau* underground as stuffy and old hat), and a spate of instant journals that came on the scene in the late 1960s and early 1970s to service the "movement" on the college campuses and among the street people in metropolitan communities. And, as Nelson points out, "They are anything but objective. They argue that true objectivity is a myth, anyway. To them, news is a four-letter word."[2]

If the tone of the long-established opinion journals is serious, that of the underground press is shrill, mocking, furious. The writers deal in logical argument as little as they do in news; their specialties are name-calling and the other devices of the propagandist. They speak, of course, to those of like ideological convictions, so concern with balance, evidence, and reasoning is unimportant to them. They defend their tactics as necessary to right an imbalance created and long nourished by the establishment press, and this has apparently constituted an appealing and sufficient philosophy for some young writers who have cast their lot with the underground press and its tactics.

THE COLUMNISTS

If the opinion journals—all shades—are reincarnations of the pamphlets and broadsides of an earlier era, the syndicated columnists of today could perhaps be described as the inheritors of the role of the thunderers of the nineteenth century—the Greeleys and Pulitzers who commanded wide personal followings and influence.

Whereas a century ago one reader talking to another might have asked, "Did you see what Greeley said about . . . ?" today his counterpart might be asking "Did you see what Alsop (or Kilpatrick) said about . . . ?" or perhaps, "Did you see what the *Times* said about . . . ?" But hardly anyone would be likely to ask, "Did you see what Oakes said about . . . ?" even though John Oakes is the editor of the nation's most prestigious newspaper. As was pointed out earlier, today's editor is not the widely known figure that his predecessors were. If anyone has inherited Greeley's mantle it is the syndicated columnist or TV commentator.

In addition to recognition and following, the columnist enjoys greater freedom than does his colleague laboring unknown and unsung on the anonymous editorial sections of the newspapers and magazines. In effect, the syndicated columnist is an entrepreneur, selling his column (or having it sold for him by the syndicate's salesmen) to anywhere from 100 to 500 editors. He determines the character and content of his column and hopes that it will prove interesting enough to a sufficient number of editorial clients (and their readers) so that he can be economically successful.

Thus in a sense he writes his own ticket—so long as he can continue to produce a salable product. He does not have to fit into the policy framework of a given newspaper (except for those columnists such as James Reston who are members of an individual newspaper staff and whose columns are written at least partly for that paper).

Also, because he does have a personal following and typically has managed to establish his credentials with that following, he may not have to spell out his evidence and argumentation as painstakingly as the newspaper editorial writer. As we noted in Chapter 7 in a quotation from a Roscoe Drummond column, he can venture far out on flimsy limbs with predictions unsupported by back-up statistics or even logic.

Yet the columnists do not deal only in such coin. Most of them are former reporters or editorial writers and continue to function in part as newsmen (Rowland Evans and Robert Novak are representative of that category). And all of them from time to time offer evidence, witnesses, and argumentation, even as their colleagues on the left side of the page.

Note this lead from a James Kilpatrick column, using an anecdotal opening and an argument from analogy (he continues to be an editorial writer as well as columnist):

> King Pyrrhus of Epirus, late in life, took on the Romans at Asculum. He won the battle, or so it is said, but he lost all his men. "One more such victory," said the King, coining the immortal phrase, "and I am lost."
>
> Pyrrhus was an old pro among the Greek warriors of his day. By the time he got to Asculum, he had won a few and lost a few, and he had a feel for these things. In the statue most frequently depicted, he looks pretty tired. So, too, with Richard Nixon. Over the past few weeks, he has recorded a string of putative victories. But a few more like these, and the old pro is done for.[3]

The columnist who relys exclusively on expressions of personal opinion may not long retain his following; he has to back up his views with something solid in the way of evidence or argumentation at least part of the time. (Barry Goldwater, the politician, and John O'Hara, the novelist, both did only moderately well as syndicated columnists because they relied too heavily on top-of-the-head opinion and too little on back-up substance.)

HOW EDITORS USE COLUMNISTS

In theory, the syndicated columnists provide the editors of the nation's newspapers with a kind of smorgasbord of opinion offerings from which to choose. The editors can pick from the array with one of several objectives in mind: (1) to bring to their editorial pages the liveliest and most interesting viewpoints available; (2) to bring to their pages columnists whose political ideology *reinforces* that of the newspaper's own editorials; or (3) to bring to their pages columnists whose ideology *counterbalances* the newspaper's own policy line.

Ben. H. Bagdikian, a press critic who later became national news editor of the *Washington Post,* made a study of the way in which columnists were used on daily newspapers representing more than half of the newspaper circulation in the country. He found that 61 percent of the papers in his sample carried an imbalance of columnists whose views *coincided* with the editorial position of the newspaper, 20 percent carried a balanced set, and 19 percent carried an imbalance of columnists whose views *differed* from those of the newspaper. In other words, nearly two-thirds of the editors were using the columnists to reinforce the newspaper's own position, and only one-fifth could be said to be trying to counterbalance their own editorial stands by publishing columnists with opposing views.[4]

In another analysis published two years later (in 1966), however, Bagdikian reported that not only was there evident a dramatic increase in the number of syndicated columnists being used, but

> similarly striking is growth of the idea that a paper should give a voice to "the other side." The degree of this shift toward the liberal side is overstated by using large metropolitan papers because it is precisely these big-city dailies that have shifted most vigorously, while smaller papers, as confirmed by syndicate operators and by sampling, tend to remain very conservative. Nevertheless, the shift is dramatic.[5]

It should be observed in passing that any attempt to categorize columnists along a liberal-conservative spectrum is necessarily imprecise and speculative. Bagdikian used editors as evaluators. The data on which his two articles were based were, however, well-aged at the time. A more recent effort to get an evaluation of the liberal-conservative leanings of contemporary columnists was made at the 1970 meeting of the National Conference of Editorial Writers (NCEW). Donald W. Carson of the University of Arizona distributed to the NCEW members in attendance a questionnaire asking them to list, among other things, the "best liberal spokesmen," "best conservative spokesmen," and "best reporters" among currently published columnists.

Some of the leaders, as the NCEW members evaluated them, were:

Best liberal spokesmen—James Reston, 23; Tom Wicker, 15; Joseph Kraft, 14; Marquis Childs, 9; Carl T. Rowan and John Roche, 7 each; Mary McGrory, 6; Clayton Fritchey and Frank Mankiewicz-Tom Braden, 4 each; Max Lerner, 3; Joseph Alsop and Rowland Evans-Robert Novak, 2 each.

Best conservative spokesmen—James J. Kilpatrick, 32; William F. Buckley, 30; William S. White, 7; Holmes Alexander, 6; David Lawrence, 5; Richard Wilson and Russell L. Kirk, 4 each; Jenkin Lloyd Jones, 3; the Drummonds, 2.

Best reporters—Rowland Evans-Robert Novak, 29; Jack Anderson, 15; Victor Riesel, 7; David Broder, 6; Frank Mankiewicz-Tom Braden, 4; Mary McGrory, Clark Mollenhoff, Jim Bishop, Joseph Alsop, the Drummonds [Roscoe and Geoffrey], and Bruce Boisatt, 2 each.[6]

However they are picked, the syndicated columnists seem to enjoy a trusting reception from the readers—in fact, they are sometimes considered more trustworthy than the papers in which they appear.

A 1970 study made on behalf of the Associated Press Managing Editors Association involved interviews with a representative sample of respondents from throughout the country. Among the questions asked was this one: "Which do you find more reliable, columnists or newspaper editorials?" The response came out this way:

Columnists more reliable	31%
Newspaper editorials more reliable	23%
No difference	36%
Other response, or no answer	10%[7]

Some editors, though, do not have as good an opinion of the columnists as many of their readers have. Several of the respondents to the

Carson survey of NCEW members indicated that they felt columnists have little value today. And long-time publisher Mark Ethridge of the *Louisville Courier-Journal* wrote a few years ago:

> Some of them [the columnists] still rock along, but it seems to me, maybe because I am getting on in years, that the liberals are tired and the conservatives tiresome. There is more pontificating, more griping, more off-the-cuff reflection and less digging and certainly less contribution to public thought.
>
> Under the luminous Kennedy and the wily Johnson, both certainly men of action, there has been a proliferation of columnists —occasionally a fresh breeze, such as my old debate—mate James Jackson Kilpatrick, the best of the conservative columnists—but at the same time I think there has been a dimunition of their influence. A *Fortune* study of a few years ago showed that only 10 per cent of those polled took their opinions from columnists, whereas both radio commentators and newspaper editorialists ranked much higher.[8]

Just for balance, we might add here an evaluation of newspaper editorials by one of those columnists, James J. Kilpatrick:

> "A vast quantity of editorials—perhaps half of all those published —are of a dullness that makes a man weep; they are pontifical, portentous, pointless; their writers boil not, neither do they grin. They merely plod. Many other editorials suffer from a kind of grotesque cuteness, like a nursery cap on a basset hound. Still others repel the rational reader with the porcupine quills of bang-marks: Hoffa must go! Labor must be curbed! Down with fluoridation!"

That's only a partial quote, and later on Kilpatrick did acknowledge that "Yet, when full account has been given to these abominations, it still seems to me that by and large, the quality of writing is better [than 20 years ago.]"[9] But still. . . .

LABELED AND UNLABELED

Another vehicle through which the opinion function is wielded is the general circulation magazine, particularly the newsmagazine. It is not easy to make the case that the opinion section of general circulation magazines constitutes a distinctive category, since there are overlaps with categories already discussed. Columnists, for example, appear in magazines as well as newspapers, and some columnists are themselves editors of general circulation magazines (David Lawrence both edited *U.S. News & World Report* and authored a widely syndicated column). Also, the general circulation magazine in some respects resembles the newspaper in that it appeals to a broad general audience (unlike the small, specialized circle that is the audience of the opinion journal) and offers a variety of wares, not just opinion.

Because there are these resemblances and overlaps, we can deal quickly with that aspect of the opinion function in the general magazines that is openly labeled as such. The essay-editorials in *Time* or other magazines differ very little from newspaper editorials, except that the magazine writers sometimes have more space to work with (*Time*'s typical essay is a double-truck; i.e., two facing pages).

But the opinion function is evident in the magazines not only above the surface but also below it. And as with the iceberg, the unseen part may be the more significant.

Using a variety of devices, writers for the general circulation newsmagazines can build a slant into what on the surface appears to be a straight news account. *Time* has been singled out for criticism for this offense more than *Newsweek, U.S. News,* or *National Observer*, and probably rightly. John C. Merrill of the University of Missouri concluded after a study of *Time*'s political reporting that the magazine "editorialized in its regular news columns to a great extent," making use of "a whole series of tricks to bias the stories and to lead the reader's thinking." [10]

These tricks include deck-stacking (focusing on selected details of a given news situation and thus conveying a partially true impression) and term-shifting (praising an attitude or action by a *Time* hero of the moment, while ridiculing the same attitude or action if it involves a current *Time* villain). During the mid-1960s *Time* was strongly in favor of American involvement in Vietnam ("It's the right war in the right place at the right time," said associate editor and chief war writer, Jason McManus), [11] and much of its handling of news of that war was tailored to support the magazine's position. Later, *Time*'s editors became disenchanted with the interminable conflict and the treatment of the news shifted.

In recent years, most observers agree, *Time* has displayed less bias in its news handling than it did during Henry Luce's lifetime. And *Newsweek,* which in earlier years had been considered to offend less often than *Time* in peddling unlabeled opinion, has lately been letting its liberal editorial philosophy show through in its news columns. The third of the big three newsmagazines, *U.S. News & World Report,* relies on charts, graphs, interviews, and purported news stories. Of this magazine, Roy Paul Nelson observes:

> Despite its devotion to conservatism, the magazine enjoys a reputation for objectivity. The reputation is not altogether deserved. Its stories are written in straightforward newspaper style, yes. But the reader soon discovers that the stories played up, the angles covered, tend to make the point that "liberalism" (the magazine likes to put it in quote marks) and centralization of government are ruining the country. Alone among major magazines, *USNWR* has represented the Southern point of view on the subject of integration and Negro rights. [12]

To whatever degree it is done, and by whatever sleight of hand it is accomplished, the introduction of *unlabeled* opinion into the content of the mass media constitutes a deception of the reader. But it would be very wrong to leave the impression that unlabeled opinion is hawked only by the newsmagazines; it is also very much a part of daily journalism, both print and broadcast.

THE "NOW" ("NEW"?) JOURNALISM

For four decades journalists and observers and critics of journalism have been wrangling among themselves and in more public forums over an issue that has been given various labels from time to time. The labels have sometimes constituted editorial evaluations of the merits of one side or another in the debate: "false objectivity *vs.* interpretive reporting" was one such tag; "slanting the news *vs.* reporting the facts," was another. In recent years we have been hearing about "journalism of advocacy," or the "new journalism," or the "now journalism."

The argument at the center of this long-continuing and multilabeled discussion is an important and complicated one. It strains the scope of this book to get very deeply into it, and yet it is germane to any consideration of the opinion function. So let's explore it for a bit.

The issue first surfaced in the 1930s, with a plea from some journalists and observers for more effort to explain the complexities of the news. Henry Luce and Briton Hadden had started *Time* in the 1920s and a decade later it was a proven success, operating on the assumption that the reader was bewildered by much of the news and wasn't getting enough help in understanding it. *Time* offered a predigested, interpreted version of the news and found a lively market for its offering.

The daily journalists, some argued, ought to be able to do the same sort of thing. And besides, the concept of "objective" news reporting that had come to be the guiding ethic of the newsrooms was getting a skeptical second look from many newsmen. What is a "fact" anyway, and how "objective" can any human be in sorting out true facts from not-so-true ones? In professing to be providing an objective news report, they asked, are we foisting a fraud on the public (particularly when there were still Hearsts, McCormicks, and others around to provide examples of editors who flew the banner of objectivity but regularly stacked the decks in their "news" columns)?

The notion of interpretive reporting gained further support some years later when, in the days of the late Sen. Joseph R. McCarthy, it became clear how easily an agile demagogue could take advantage of the kind of objectivity that treated any observation from a United States senator as automatic and important news. Here, certainly, the advocates of interpretation argued, was proof that we must go behind the myth of objectivity. They cited the finding of the Hutchins Commission on a Free and Responsible Press (1947) to the effect that "it is no longer enough to report the *fact* truthfully. It is now necessary to report the *truth about the fact.*"

So, heeding the injunction, a good many newspapermen set out to find not facts, but the truth (a quest that had been baffling the world's philosophers for three millenia). They sought to illuminate the truth in the news by supplementing the surface facts with additional ones dredged up out of background or history; with the quoted opinions of persons with a right to be heard on the subject under discussion; and, finally, with some generous helpings of their *own* opinion and evaluation of what a given event meant or how sincere a given newsmaker really was.

Many editors saw in this an unfortunate trend. They warned against permitting editorializing and slanting to creep into the news columns under a mask of respectability. They pointed out that "interpretation" may be one thing in the hands of an experienced and deeply informed reporter who knows his news beat intimately and quite a different matter when it is practiced by every Tom, Dick, and Harry in the newsroom—most of whom may have little or no qualifications for judging the motives and meanings in the news events they report.

During the time of ferment in the late 1960s and early 1970s, the long persisting debate took on new dimensions. One was introduced by such writers as Truman Capote, Tom Wolfe, and Gay Talese, who brought to the reporting of news the arts and artifices of the fiction writer. They would steep themselves in their subject, literally live with an interviewee for months. (Capote spent *years* developing the understanding that he built into his book, *In Cold Blood,* an intensive, minutely detailed, highly interpretive report of a mass murder and the two murderers.) And they would write not in conventional news prose, but with stylistic flourishes out of the novelist's repertoire—and with some other of the novelist's devices as well, including reconstructed dialogue and mind reading.

Another new dimension came with the pressure for change that was expressed by the minority, activist, and alienated groups—the blacks, the college generation, the Women's Liberation movement. These groups found advocates in journalism, who insisted that so many changes had to be made so quickly that the mass media of communication must put their vast leverage to the task. Through many generations, they argued, the newspapers and other media had put their weight on the scales on the side of things as they were, the status quo. Now, to right the imbalance long maintained, journalists must step out of the role of reporter and into that of advocate—in the news columns as well as on the editorial pages.

Dr. J. K. Hvistendahl, a journalism educator, called the new development a fourth revolution in journalism. (The first revolution, he said, was the freeing of the press from government control; the second was the growth of the objective press; and the third was the rise of interpretive reporting).

Now the fourth revolution is upon us, and the revolutionists are activist reporters. The journalistic activist believes he has a right (indeed an obligation) to become personally and emotionally involved in the events of the day. He believes he should proclaim his beliefs if he wishes, and that it is not only permissible but desirable for him to cover the news from the viewpoint of his own intellectual commitment. He looks at traditional reporting as being sterile, and he considers reporters who refuse to commit themselves to a point of view as being cynical or hypocritical. The activist believes that attempting to describe the events of a complicated world objectively seldom results in the truth for anybody—the source, the reporter, or the reader or listener. . . . "Truth-as-I-see-it" reporting, rather than activist reporting, might be a more accurate description of the fourth revolution. The new reporters don't claim that they, or anybody else, have a corner on the truth. But they insist that the reporter, like the scientist, has an obligation to report the truth as he sees it. . . . Truth-as-I-see-it reporting is not editorializing. It is an honest attempt on the part of the reporter to bring together all the material that he can on a subject on which he has strong feelings. The article may be one-sided, or it may be balanced. Perhaps his decision is to make no decision. But is is an honest attempt to seek the truth. If the reporter is honest, he will be accurate, and he will be fair. But he'll follow the information he has to its logical conclusion, and make judgments, if judgment seems apparent to him. [13]

The new journalism concept, enunciated in various ways by its advocates and practitioners, brought the debate over objectivity to a new level of intensity, four decades after it had begun. Eric Sevareid, in an observation delivered on his 30th anniversary in the broadcasting industry, said:

> Now among some of the earnest young, a different concept of journalism is developing. Mission-oriented journalism, they call it—commitment to cause or doctrine . . . based on the proposition that objective reporting or explanation of the news does not exist, since all reporters are human and conditioned one way or another. We used to call this propaganda. [14]

And one of Sevareid's part-time colleagues, Theodore H. White, who is also a novelist and occasional newsmagazine reporter, described what consequences can flow from embracing the doctrine of mission-oriented journalism:

> I did the movie version of *The Making of the President 1968.* We had two crews on the road all the time. They were young and wonderful cameramen. I was busy writing my book and reporting and I couldn't direct the film crews, so about nine months later when I finally got to Hollywood to put the film together, I found that these young people absolutely adored Eugene McCarthy and Robert Kennedy, and there was not a bad shot of either Gene McCarthy or Bobby Kennedy in the thousands and thousands of feet that we took. The images were glowing. On the other hand, these people who worked with me did not bring back one human shot of Hubert Humphrey. Everything that was taken looked sinister. He has an angular face, a pointed chin, and if you want to shoot Hubert badly, it's the easiest thing in the world. I have a personal fondness for Hubert Humphrey. I have known him for fifteen years. But I had to work with a film that showed Hubert Humphrey only as a sinister character. Such problems are even

more pointed when you come to the daily TV shows. You're in the hands of the hundreds of people who are feeding material to you. [15]

And yet another critical assessment of the latest trend in interpretive journalism was offered by Ray Stephens, assistant chief of the Associated Press bureau at Washington, D.C., in a speech given at the Pennsylvania Press Conference:

> The catchwords and phrases of the New Journalists betray their real concern. They are not content to be observers. They are determined to exert an influence, to be opinion makers. They talk about the importance of what reporters think, of the reporter's right to take a moral stance, to have firm convictions and to express them in print. Always beware of a man who talks in terms of "moral commitment." Invariably he is a man who has totally bought the line peddled by the advocates of one cause or another. . . . If I believe anything, it is this: Any man who begins an examination of any subject armed with a set of preconceptions will tend to exaggerate the significance of evidence he finds to support his point of view, and denigrate the significance of that data which tends to contradict him. [16]

And the debate will undoubtedly continue for some time to come. The arguments of the advocates of one side or the other are themselves casemaking, of course. The reader of this book by now should be able to analyze and assess the quality of the case making for himself. For example, there is some question begging by Hvistendahl. He says that the new journalists "insist that the reporter, like the scientist, has an obligation to report the truth as he sees it." But does the scientist report the truth as he sees it or the truth *as he finds it* by application of the scientific method? Is the analogy sound? Or, to cite a failing in the other camp, look back at Stephens: "Always beware of a man who talks in terms of 'moral commitment.' Invariably he is a man who has totally bought the line peddled by the advocates of one cause or another." *Invariably?* Is that sweeping generalization acceptable?

But however long the debate goes on, one conclusion is inescapable: Unlabeled opinion is being sold every day to the reader or viewer of the mass media, whether it is under the guise of interpretive reporting or journalism of advocacy, whether it is below the by-line of John Jones or Norman Mailer. And the question of whether the reader is fairly served by this practice is a troubling one.

The *Wall Street Journal,* which carries some excellent "background" or interpretive reporting in its pages, took a look recently at the degree to which the tactics of new journalism have been accepted by magazine and newspaper writers. The article took particular note of the device of the composite character, someone presented in an article as an actual person, quoted and described, but who doesn't exist as an individual. He is made up of quotes and parts from a good many persons who actually were interviewed and whose quotes are correct—except that they are all attributed to the composite, the protagonist of the story. The *Wall Street Journal* reporter referred to an article in *New York* magazine about a hustler named "Redpants," whose life is intimately described and whose philosophy is reflected in the candid quotations included in the article. But there was no real Redpants; she was a composite character. And the *Journal* reporter continued:

> So the story was true, sort of, but then again it wasn't. The reader, however, was not told any of this.
>
> It's all part of the New Journalism, or the Now Journalism, and it's practiced widely these days. Some editors and reporters vigorously defend it. Others just as vigorously attack it. No one has polled the reader, but whether he approves or disapproves it's getting harder and harder for him to know what he can believe. For example:
>
> ■ *Esquire* some time ago ran a cover showing the reclusive Howard Hughes, but it wasn't really Howard Hughes. And in another issue, right in the middle of a long piece on the war, there was a whole chunk of made-up dialog between the author and a made-up U.S. general. The reader was never told what was fact and what was fiction, or, indeed, that there was any fiction in the piece at all.
> ■ *Philadelphia* magazine in May 1969 ran an astonishingly detailed account of a burglar named Harry Phillips and his pal, Joey, detailing how they robbed the home of a wealthy Main Line doctor. Harry, the magazine disclosed, has been arrested four times and once served a six-month sentence in Delaware County. One additional fact, which the readers weren't told, is that Harry and Joey are composite characters.
> ■ And, as the world now knows, the *National Review* published some "secret papers" that came not from the Pentagon but rather from the fertile mind of William Buckley, the urbane editor.

Newspapers and broadcasters handled the "papers" as if they were news, and Mr. Buckley didn't own up to his prank until after publication.

All this raises some questions that are beginning to trouble practitioners and nonpractitioners alike. To what extent should such techniques as using composite characters be employed? If used extensively, do they edge a story into the fiction category? Is an editor obliged to alert the reader? And to what extent does the "new journalism" strain the credibility of the author or the publication or the profession in general? This last question is perhaps the most important.[17]

The *Journal* reporter is undoubtedly correct in his last statement. For if the credibility of the media with the public dwindles away, all of their effort—whether to inform or to influence—will be wasted. The widespread introduction of the opinion function into the news-disseminating aspects of the mass media could result in such an erosion of credibility; in fact, there is some evidence that the erosion is already underway.

A survey of newspaper readers earlier cited in this chapter included some questions dealing with this point. One of them asked the respondents: "Newspapers say that they express their own opinions only in editorials but never in the news columns. Do you . . . ?

Strongly agree	5%
Agree	36%
Disagree	41%
Strongly disagree	10%
Other, or no answer	9%

Thus more than half of the readers questioned indicated their belief that opinion was seeping into the news columns. Another question in the same interview was: "Do you feel these [the newspaper's] editorial stands have any effect on the news stories in your papers?"

Yes	49%
No	30%
Other, no answer	11%[18]

However, let's note again—this is far from a new issue. It has been around for a long while and promises to remain on the scene for some time to come.

OPINION ON THE AIR

One final specialized utilization of the opinion function remains to be discussed—that of the broadcast media. Opinion appears in various forms on the broadcast media, just as it does in newspapers and magazines, and some close analogies can be drawn between print and broadcast.

The analysis provided by commentators such as Eric Sevareid can be compared directly with the work of the newspaper columnist. The exhaustive examination of a single topic on a network documentary program is very much like the kind of interpretive coverage given in a newspaper series or a lengthy magazine article. And the *Time*-style unlabeled opinion also has its counterpart on the air in the newscaster who, by the inflection of his voice, the expression on his face, or the angle of his eyebrow, can build as effective a slant into a news item as could any newsmagazine specialist or advocacy journalist.

But the opinion writer for radio or television—particularly television—has to contend with some problems that his colleagues in the editorial offices of the print media do not face. The newspaper editorial writer or the magazine columnist has a fairly simple, direct line to his audience; to be sure, he must usually go through some editing checkpoint (on a magazine, perhaps several of them), but otherwise he has a relatively uncomplicated procedural path to follow once he has an idea worked out and is ready to go to work at his typewriter.

Life isn't so simple for the opinion writer for television. He may have to work with numerous persons, including technicians. He may have to tailor his writing to fit the equipment he must use to reach his audience. (Theodore H. White once observed that working with television is like trying to write with a twelve-ton pen.)

Most trying of all, perhaps, is the tight wordage limit within which he must try to accomplish his objectives. Robert Novak, the syndicated newspaper columnist, also writes and delivers 15-minute columns for broadcast. His approach differs considerably from medium to medium. Whereas he can develop several moderately complex thoughts in a single newspaper column, he says that he can handle only one idea in a radio column with roughly the same number of words. He is obliged to repeat the central theme to be sure that he is getting it across effectively; in print, he can set the idea out once and then couple it with other ideas or with backstop evidence.[19]

HOW MUCH IN TWO MINUTES?

Even more challenging is the assignment of the broadcast opinion writer who is the counterpart of the newspaper editorialist. Novak was talking about the limitations that the 15-minute time block imposed on him as a columnist; the editorial writer for radio or television—again, particularly for television—typically has only *two* minutes, not 15, within which to accomplish his objectives. Most station managers are reluctant to allocate larger time blocks to editorial commentary.

Direct editorializing—as distinguished from the commentator-columnist role or the approach of the background documentary—is handled on broadcasting stations as a management function. As on the newspaper, the point of view expressed is that of the station management, not of any individual. Thus most broadcast editorials are delivered by the manager or his representative, even though they may have been written by an editorial writer.

Dr. Frank Stanton, president of the Columbia Broadcasting System, once explained to a congressional committee how the opinion function is exercised in various degrees by broadcasters:

> Although some critics of contemporary journalism, printed as well as electronic, seem to see some confusion between what is analysis and what is editorial, CBS has a working definition of each.
>
> Analysis, or interpretation, consists in an experienced reporter's going behind and beyond an event to explain its context, how it happened, why it happened, and probable repercussions. Analysis is concerned with things as they are, or as they were, or, judging from present facts, what they probably will be. An editorial is concerned with things as they ought to be. But such a judgment is forbidden to CBS reporters on the air, who may not editorialize; this judgment is reserved to management, who assumes direct responsibility for it and to whom that responsibility is directly ascribed on the air.
>
> CBS turns the analysis of news over to experienced news reporters whose judgment and insight it respects. . . . If the analysis goes over the border into editorializing, corrective steps are taken on the grounds that editorializing is a management and not an individual responsibility.[20]

Prior to 1949, broadcasters were denied the right to utilize the opinion function in any form. The position of the Federal Communications Commission (FCC) had been that "the broadcaster cannot be an advocate" because he was using a public resource—the limited number of available channels—under license. But in a 1949 ruling, the FCC reversed itself and authorized, even encouraged, broadcasters to engage in editorializing.

At first the broadcasters ventured only occasionally and cautiously into the field of labeled opinion, perhaps wanting to make sure that the FCC really meant it this time. It was not until 1954, five years after the ruling opened the way to editorializing, that WMCA in New York became the first radio station to institute regular editorial comment. And the first regularly-scheduled TV editorials did not make their appearance until 1957, on WTVJ in Miami, Florida.[21]

During those first years, editorials on the air tended to focus on innocuous subjects. As one writer put it:

> With a few notable exceptions, most stations got into the field with some caution, and editorials championing motherhood and demanding fearlessly that Main Street's name be changed to Affluent Way were more the rule than the exception.[22]

The broadcasters' caution was understandable in the circumstances. That same FCC ruling that had flashed the green light for editorializing had spelled out some guidelines that all broadcasters were expected to observe. One of these guidelines provided that, if the broadcaster aired an opinion on any controversial public issue, he must afford that issue "fair and balanced treatment."

Such fairness and balance, said the FCC, could best be achieved if the broadcaster affirmatively aided and encouraged the ventilation of opposing points of view. The practical effect of this provision has been that any editorial broadcast on radio or television must not only be specifically identified as an expression of management opinion, but should also include an invitation to opponents to offer a rebuttal of the views advanced by the editorial. Ideally, since a listener or viewer may tune in at any time, the label and the invitation should both precede and follow the editorial comment itself, thus cutting into the time available for case making. Moreover, any comment on a controversial topic implies a lien on future air time at least equivalent to the time block occupied by the editorial (and if the controversy is multifaceted, there may be a demand for rebuttal time by more than one faction, thus compounding the problem).

A study of television editorials carried out in 1969 by C. William Platt of the University of Iowa found that nearly half of the stations that editorialize extend to their viewers a "direct invitation to reply," while others make less obvious compliance with the FCC guideline. The researcher found, however, that only 6.2 percent of the stations averaged at least one audience response a week; nearly a third of them received no audience responses at all to their editorials during the month-long period of the study. He also found that most stations editorialize about five days a week, and that a given editorial is typically presented twice during the broadcast day (although a few stations will repeat an editorial as many as four or more times during the program day in an effort to reach as wide an audience as possible.)[23]

The space problem confronting the broadcast editorial writer can best be illustrated by quoting the text of an editorial delivered over television. This one was presented by Station KTVU, Channel 2, San Francisco-Oakland.

The text below is that of the editorial comment itself; in addition, there is a standard five-second opening and a seven-second closing identifying the content of "Outlook" as "editorial opinion broadcast periodically by KTVU Television" and serving as a "focus for this station's areas of concern within the community it serves." Both opening and closing comments also indicate that "your comments on editorial content are invited."

18-Year-Old Vote   Playdate: 8/13/71.

Where does an 18 year-old register to vote?

There's a problem concerning this question. Some towns, and particularly small towns which have large colleges within them, might suddenly find that elections are dominated by the temporary visitors, to the detriment of the town.

We think that's unfair, and we have a suggestion. College students should register to vote in their hometowns. If they are not in their hometowns on election day, they can vote by absentee ballot, just as all of us must do if we're away from home on that important day.

The other way—we think—is unfair.

The editorials presented on "Outlook" are delivered by Roger D. Rice, general manager of the station and vice president of Cox Broadcasting Co., and written by Deacon Anderson, editorial director of the station.

The whole of the "Outlook" broadcast, including the five-second opening and seven-second closing, takes one minute. Rice says that he prefers using the one-minute format (about half the time of the average TV editorial) because it is brief enough to be dropped into the program schedule a number of times during the day; he can present the editorial half a dozen times, sometimes with newscasts but at other times between scheduled shows in place of a commercial spot. In that way he can put the editorial before all the various audience segments of the broadcast day—and of course those segments vary greatly from one time period to the next. Longer editorials can be worked in only with newscasts.

As to the way in which editorial ideas are developed for the "Outlook" broadcasts, Rice says:

> We get our ideas for editorials through the two to four times a week community leaders' luncheons which we hold in the WTVU conference room with leaders from the overall community. For these luncheons we have congressmen, senators, college presidents, radical leaders, citizens for law and order, black leaders, Chinese leaders, student body presidents, etc. At each luncheon we spend one and a half to two hours discussing the problems of that particular segment of the community. Out of these come many ideas for editorials. Other ideas come from the news department.[24]

Rice contends that his "Outlook" editorials very likely reach a much wider audience than the editorial comment of any of the newspapers in the San Francisco Bay Area, which is his station's market. Each editorial is repeated often enough so that the station's day-long, changing audience is exposed to it. And, as he points out, the broadcast editorial is to some extent forced on the attention of the viewer, while the newspaper reader must make a special effort to turn to the right section and look for the editorials.

The one-minute format employed by KTVU is not, of course, the only packaging used for broadcast opinion. On radio, more so than on television, large time blocks are utilized. Some of the major network anchor men who stick to interpretive reporting on TV are heard on radio in 5- or 10-minute commentaries that are frankly editorial in nature. In the early 1970s, the CBS radio network developed a daily series of editorial commentary spots about three minutes in length and featuring in rotation a stable of nine widely known print journalists, ranging across the ideological spectrum from M. Stanton Evans on the Right to Murray Kempton on the Left. Both the network and the local station disavowed any identification with the views offered by these commentators, and their role was more analagous to that of the newspaper columnist than to that of the editorial writer for the print media.

In the late 1960s and early 1970s, more and more individual stations also were making effective use of editorials—and not only in the form of one- or two-minute spots. WMAQ-TV in Chicago drew so much response to a vigorous editorial comment on the Vietnam War in 1970 that the station was able to put together two *90-minute* programs, aired on successive Sunday afternoons and made up entirely of filmed viewer responses to the original editorial commentary. [25]

The number of responses received by WMAQ-TV to its single editorial broadcast (there were 11,094 letters, cards, or telephone calls) indicated that in specific instances on-the-air editorializing is capable of achieving a much broader impact than was suggested by the findings of the Platt study cited earlier in this chapter.

The potentiality for even greater leverage for broadcast opinion in all of its various forms lies in the rapidly expanding cable television systems. The time straitjacket that limits the broadcast opinion writer at the present derives from the scarcity of broadcast channels. But when cable systems are in operation, the typical present-day choice of half a dozen viewing channels can at once be expanded to twenty, forty, or even more. And as Stuart F. Sucherman points out in the *Columbia Journalism Review:*

> This aspect of cable is only the beginning of the potential of a true "wired nation." By installing a strip of copper wire within an insulating sheath only slightly larger in diameter than a lipstick tube, one can bring to every home two-way, broad-band communications that can provide a whole galaxy of new services. These could encompass facsimile reproduction of documents, including possibly newspapers, magazines, and specialized information services; computer links and data transmission affording access to information banks at libraries, medical centers, etc.; home fire and crime protection systems; and delivery of medical welfare and other social services presently dependent on outmoded institutional methods. As FCC Commissioner Nicholas Johnson once stated, "coaxial cable is to a telephone what Niagara Falls is to a garden hose." [26]

When that Niagara is fully hooked up and flowing, the whole complexion of the opinion function in the broadcast media may undergo striking changes. We'll be speculating about some of those possibilities in Chapter 14.

NOTES

1. John L. Hulteng and Roy Paul Nelson, *The Fourth Estate*, New York, Harper & Row, 1971, p. 202.

2. *Ibid.*, p. 203.

3. James J. Kilpatrick, from his column released for publication on August 10, 1971, by the Washington Star Syndicate.

4. Ben H. Bagdikian, "How Newspapers Use Columnists," *Columbia Journalism Review*, Fall 1964, pp. 20-24.

5. Ben H. Bagdikian, "How Editors Pick Columnists," *Columbia Journalism Review*, Spring 1966, pp. 40-45.

6. Donald W. Carson, "What Editorial Writers Think of Columnists," *Masthead*, Spring 1971, pp. 1-5.

7. Reported in *News Research Bulletin* No. 21, American Newspaper Publishers Association, November 19, 1970, p. 74.

8. Mark Ethridge, "The Come-Back of Editorial Pages," *Masthead*, Summer 1966, pp. 28-32.

9. James J. Kilpatrick, "A Good Page Is an Honorable Product of the Creative Art," *Bulletin of the American Society of Newspaper Editors*, October 1, 1966, pp. 3-4.

10. John C. Merrill, quoted in "The News Mags: *Time, Newsweek* Vie with Polished Prose and Reams of Research," by A. Kent Mac-Dougall, *Wall Street Journal*, July 12, 1967, pp. 1 and 13.

11. *Ibid.*, p. 1.

12. Hulteng and Nelson, *op. cit.* p. 179.

13. J. K. Hvistendahl, "The Reporter as Activist: A Fourth Revolution in Journalism," *Quill*, February 1970, pp. 8-11.

14. Quoted in *Seminar*, March 1970, p. 17.

15. Theodore H. White, "America's Two Cultures," *Columbia Journalism Review*, Winter 1969-1970, pp. 8-13.

16. Quoted in *Editor and Publisher*, June 13, 1970, p. 24.

17. W. Stewart Pinkerton, Jr., "Believe It or Not: The 'New Journalism' Is Sometimes Less Than Meets the Eye," *Wall Street Journal*, August 13, 1971, pp. 1 and 19.

18. *News Research Bulletin, op. cit.*, p. 72. The figures do not add up to 100 percent, but they are reproduced here as originally reported in the study.

19. Paraphrased from comments made by Robert Novak in a speech at Stanford University on January 26, 1971.

20. From a statement by Frank Stanton before the Subcommittee on

Communications and Power of the House Interstate and Foreign Commerce Committee, July 18, 1963.

21. William A. Wood, *Electronic Journalism*, New York, Columbia University Press, 1967, p. 62.

22. *Ibid.*, p. 65.

23. C. William Platt, "Television Editorials and Response Opportunities," *Journalism Quarterly*, Autumn 1971, pp. 500–503.

24. In a letter to the author dated August 24, 1971.

25. Marvin Barrett, editor, *Survey of Broadcast Journalism, 1969-1970*, New York, Grosset & Dunlap, 1970, p. 28.

26. Stuart F. Sucherman, "Cable TV: The Endangered Revolution," *Columbia Journalism Review*, May–June 1971, pp. 13–20.

12
The People's Forum

An article in the *National Observer,* commenting on the increase in letters to the editor in recent years, carried the headline: "Dear Mr. Editor, You Fink!"[1] That head pithily expressed the character of the lone category of opinion content of the mass media that is not directed outward—from the publication toward the reader—but inward, as feedback.

The letters-to-the-editor sections of newspapers and magazines, and their equivalents on the broadcast media, represent a chance for at least some of the people, some of the time, to talk back to the information machines. And a chance, too, to air their views before an audience of their fellow citizens.

It was noted at the outset of this book that this provision of a people's forum constitutes an important service, perhaps as important as any that the communication media provide to their readers and viewers. The letters section is a safety valve, an outlet for diversity of opinion, sometimes a healthy corrective to the publication's own stance.

Direction of the people's forum aspect of the opinion section is in the hands of the editors or editorial writers (often it is the responsibility of a newcomer to the staff), and it is important that any would-be opinion writer understand something about the how and why of its operation.

FORUM FOR WHOM?

For instance, what about the matter of accessibility? If the letters section represents, as often is claimed, the last, best hope of the average citizen for a chance to get up on his hind legs and speak his piece to a substantial audience, how valid a hope is it? How many of those who want to get their word in actually do get the chance?

The answer depends on just what publication or channel we're talking about. A community weekly or a small daily will be able to publish all or most of the usable letters that come in (if "usable" is understood to mean those that are not obscene, libelous, or otherwise legally actionable). Not every small paper *does* publish as many letters as it receives for some of the same reasons that not every small paper has a vigorous, outspoken editorial page; a lively letters section can stir up plenty of controversy. But the volume of mail is such, and the available space is such, that the small paper *can* accommodate most of its correspondence from readers if it wishes to.

Roughly speaking, the larger the circulation of the newspaper (or magazine) the smaller the fraction of letters received that actually gets into print. A small-city daily with a circulation of from 10,000 to 30,000 can find space for from one-half to two-thirds of the usable letters received. A metropolitan paper can typically handle far less of the flow (although the *Dayton* (Ohio) *Daily News*, with a 60,000 circulation, publishes *every* letter it gets that is not obscene or libelous).

The very largest papers can publish only a small fraction of the letters input. The *New York Times,* which has a staff of six persons assigned full-time to the handling of the letters section, receives up to 40,000 letters a year and manages to get about 6 percent into print. The editor of the editorial page of the *Times,* John Oakes, says "I take the letters column of our newspaper seriously and I consider the letters to the editor as a vital counterpoint—or perhaps antidote is a better word—to the editorials themselves."[2]

The *London Times,* which constitutes perhaps the world's most prestigious platform for letter writers, receives from 80,000 to 90,000 letters a year, of which about 5,000 are published.[3]

The odds the letter writer faces are even steeper on a major magazine. *Time* publishes about 2 percent of the total of letters received, and even that select fraction goes through an extensive editing-down process before going into the letters column.

Broadcasters also limit access to the people's forum in varying degrees. WPIX in New York City presents on the air some of the 25 or 30 letters a week the station receives, but the writers are identified by initials only. A Cleveland TV station manager sifts through anywhere from 80 to 100 letters a week to prepare two feedback broadcasts including from one to four letters in each (identifying authors only by initials). The call-in shows on radio provide another kind of audience participation, again usually anonymous.

So the feedback platform is clearly not accessible to all comers, except perhaps on the very small media channels. But for those who do get a chance to occupy it, if only briefly, it is a valued outlet for pent-up frustrations or for original and interesting observations that might otherwise never have exposure.

NOT ALL KOOKS AND CRANKS

Perhaps the next logical questions are, Who are those who do get a chance at the public forum? How representative are they of the readers generally and of the public?

Some who write in are clearly on the fringes of society—and even of sanity. As one editor put it:

> Many letters come from obvious nuts. Jack Spalding, editor of the Atlanta *Journal,* says letters provide "a safety valve" for unbalanced readers. "Ramblings of obscene and evil minds" account for 25 per cent to 30 per cent of the *Journal*'s mail, he says. They're from emotionally disturbed people who don't like the world we live in and are inclined to blame us for the world's troubles—and their own." These letters never see print.[4]

The experience of other editors has not been quite so disillusioning as that of Mr. Spalding. In every editor's mailbag there is a fairly consistent incidence of obscene, hate, or crank mail. But it typically is nowhere near as high as the 25 to 30 percent mentioned by the Atlanta editor. Most letter writers are not kooks.

But neither are they representative of the community as a whole, or even of the publication's readership. A study made in 1965 at Kansas State University by G. L. Vacin of letters to the editor in Kansas newspapers indicated that most of the writers were elderly or middle-aged, most were well-educated, with 14 or more years of schooling, and most were male (3 to 1).[5]

Other similar studies have suggested that writers of letters to the editor are typically older and more conservative than the general population or the overall readership of the publication involved. They also tend to be "against" rather than "for" whatever they are writing about. It should be borne in mind, however, that these studies were made several years ago. There have been changes since then, and not only in terms of the increased volume of letters to the editor.

For one thing, the national debate over the legitimacy of the Vietnam war has brought out a far greater volume of correspondence from young people and liberals than has typically been the case in the past. This alone would mean a change in the complexion of the letter-writing segment of the readership. It is also the case that politicians and their supporters have in recent years discovered the potentialities of the letters section. This is one of the best-read parts of the newspaper. (Repeated studies reported in the *News Research for Better Newspapers* series, Volumes 1 through 5, edited by Chilton R. Bush for the American Newspaper Publishers Association Foundation, have indicated the persisting high readership scores earned by the letters section.) It also provides the politician a chance for some free space in the paper (unlike paid advertising). So there has been a substantial increase in the input of letters dealing with political candidacies, some from candidates themselves but even more from supporters who have been organized into letter-writing campaigns. The composite of the typical letter writer developed in the early studies might not at all be typical of his counterpart today.

There is also one other caveat to be noted about the profiles of letter writers that have been reported. Two Stanford scholars, David Grey and Trever Brown, pointed out that all such profiles have been drawn of the letter writers *whose letters were published,* which itself may be a distorting factor.

> More letters are apparently being written to newspapers but are they published? And is the demographic profile of the typical letter-writer changing? Since most of the 30 years research on letters-to-the-editor has been based on only those published, it may be that the profile which has emerged reflects less the writers themselves than the selection of editors. A broader but largely invisible cross-section of Americans may have been writing for some time; theirs may be the inarticulate, sometimes abusive letters screened from print. Until more systematic knowledge of editorial selection decisions is available, we may be losing valuable indicators of political attitudes, frustrations, and change.[6]

Such knowledge as we have of the bases on which editors select letters for publication comes in the form of comments or quotations from such editors now and then. The procedure on the *New York Times,* for example, is the following:

The first step is to weed out the small quota every publication receives from kooks, obscenity-slingers, publicity seekers, and do-gooders. Like Congressmen, the *Times* is frequently the object of letter-writing campaigns; these are easily detectable and generally are given little heed. . . . What he [Kalman Seigel, the letters editor] and his staff look for, he says, are letters that tie in with current news and are written by people who know their subject and present it clearly. They pass up vituperative or anonymous letters or those signed with a pseudonym, although on rare occasions they'll permit the use of initials if there's a good reason. They tend to shun "professional" letter writers, insist on exclusive publication, limit the length of a letter to a maximum of 400 to 450 words, and generally follow a policy of not printing more than two letters a year from a single contributor.[7]

Lauren K. Soth, editor of the editorial page of the *Des Moines Register and Tribune,* once observed that on his page, "We treat a contribution from a reader the same as we treat any piece of copy—on its merits as interesting, informative reading material. We edit letters, illustrate them, give them good head display."[8]

HONESTY IS THE *ONLY* POLICY

Soth's comment brings up one aspect of the handling of letters sections —for whatever medium—that is fundamental and essential. The letters must be given fair and honest treatment; this is the reader's forum and he is entitled to unbiased handling. If the readers once decide that a given letters section is stacked with puffery for the publication's positions or pet causes or that reader contributions are being mangled out of shape before being committed to print, confidence in the publication—and the volume of letters—will drop off sharply and deservedly.

The letters section is peculiarly subject to manipulation, if the editor running it has no scruples. Although he may know, and the researchers may know, that the letters section of a newspaper is not a faithful mirror of public opinion, the average reader may not be so sophisticated. He may indeed believe that the reactions he sees in the evening paper's mailbag section do represent a reflection of the community's thinking on the issues of the day.

Given this, the unscrupulous editor who wants to use the letters section as an instrument of hidden persuasion has several options open to him—none of which is subject to ready detection.

For example, suppose he is receiving a strong flow of mail on a given issue—divided about 70 percent in favor of the issue and 30 percent against it. But the paper is opposed to the issue and would like to plant the suggestion that the public is too. To accomplish this the editor need only juggle the proportions of the letters he publishes. He is able to publish only a fraction, so some selection must take place; the reader makes the assumption that the fraction published will accurately reflect the pro-con division in the whole mailbag received. But a venally inclined editor could reverse those proportions—publishing seven letters against for every three letters for the issue at stake—and present a picture of public thinking exactly opposite of the reality. And who is to catch him at it? No one audits the mailbag.

Or, if he wants to be more subtle about his skulduggery, he can publish the pro-con letters in honest proportion. But, he can carefully select those that he publishes so that all the pro letters (the side he doesn't favor) are ones that are poorly phrased, illogical, or even illiterate, while all the con letters published are smoothly edited masterpieces of logic and wisdom. He thus sets up the impression that all the community's intelligent and right-thinking people are on his side, while the confused and ignorant types are on the other.

Such practices are repugnant to the vast majority of editorial page editors, who value the letters section and who give reader contributions as careful and as fair a handling as any other copy for the page; Soth spoke for that majority. But there are also a few editors who have been known to tamper with the letters section to reinforce the paper's editorial position.

SOME GROUND RULES

There are guidelines for the conduct of a letters-to-the-editor section that are observed on most newspapers and magazines. When they are observed, the result is usually widespread public confidence in the integrity of the forum and a gratifying flow of letters—sure sign of a lively and healthy editorial page.

1. If readers' contributions must be edited for length (almost always the case) the spirit, the chief thrust of the letter writer, should never be warped or distorted. A careful editor can prune down a letter to fit the publication's space limitations without letting his knife cut into live tissue. To be sure, the reader will not want to have a single word lost, but he will be understanding if the *gist* of what he wanted to say remains intact.

2. As many individuals as possible should be provided access to the letters section; it should not become the monopoly of an elite or a prolific few. Any publication hears from regulars of various kinds, professional letter writers, members of an organized claque. Most editors ration the regulars to one appearance a month or every two months, and most try to screen out the contributions that obviously stem from a synthetic letter-writing campaign.

(Some regulars are in a special category. One such is J. Kesner Kahn, of Chicago, who since 1950 has spent about 10 hours a week writing regularly to some 100 daily and weekly newspapers.[9] Another was Charles Hooper, saluted by the *New York Times* as "Letter Writer to the World." He was an independently wealthy New Yorker who moved in 1913 to the little town of Coeur d'Alene, Idaho, and spent the rest of his life as a full-time writer of letters to the editor. He died in 1941, after producing "hundreds of thousands" of letters to editors all over the world.)[10]

3. The authenticity of all letters ought to be checked out consistently and carefully, not only to protect the writers but to safeguard the publication against embarrassment or legal liability. The letters section presents a temptation to some in the community who would like to get a fellow citizen in trouble; they forge his name to a foolish or ill-tempered letter and send it off to the paper, hoping it will be published and put the victim in hot water.

To guard against this, most editorial page editors insist that every letter be signed with the writer's name and address, and then they take special precautions to check out the signature's authenticity. Some editors send out a standard form to be signed by the writer, acknowledging that he wrote the letter and authorizing its publication. Others rely on telephone checks, to avoid the delay caused by mail exchange.

When such checking is neglected, or is not painstaking, the results can be awkward, if not worse. The *New York Times* once published a letter purportedly written by a cadet at West Point, criticizing the policies of a then prominent general. The letter was signed with the name "Grant Hall," which, as someone subsequently pointed out to the abashed *Times* editors, is the name of a dormitory at the Point. And *Time* magazine once printed a letter apparently signed by four persons from India; the names actually were obscenities in Hindi.[11] A good many libel actions have stemmed from letters to the editor that contained actionable material that had not been checked out before publication; the newspaper or magazine is fully liable for any such material, even though the author is not a member of the publication's staff.

4. The editor should not talk back to or undercut the letter writer in the letters column itself. It often happens that a letter to the editor will take the publication to task in bitter terms. If the editor wants to pick up the gauntlet and continue the argument, he should do so in his own section of the page—the editorial columns. It is a cheap put down to append a cutting rejoinder to the reader's letter, as is done on some publications.

Almost as bad is the practice of some editors in permitting staff members to intrude on the letters section, which ought to belong exclusively to the reader. Melville F. Ferguson, then editor of the *Philadelphia Bulletin,* once acknowledged:

> When subscribers fail to come across in adequate volume, some member of the staff—who has as much right to appear in print as any nonprofessional—can always be found to administer a kick to cats, dogs, women drivers or other pets of large segments of the population and start a wave of reaction.[12]

Most editorial page editors, however, reserve the letters column exclusively for genuine reader contributions. And they try, also, to observe the other guidelines cited above. In the process they earn the readers' confidence in the public forum section of the mass media.

A survey of reader attitudes conducted by the Associated Press Managing Editors Association and cited in Chapter 11 put the following question to its sample of newspaper readers from across the country: "Most newspapers do not have the space to print all reader letters they receive. Do you think your newspaper selects letters which agree with its own opinion or those which are the most worth reading?" The answers:

Agree with editors' opinion	10%
Most worth reading	77%
Other response, no answer	13%[13]

Although that question measured only one dimension of confidence,ι the answers perhaps could be taken as a more generalized reflection of readers' attitudes toward the letters section.

This feeling of confidence may be enhanced in the future, as more papers follow the lead of some in devoting still more space to letters, either on the editorial page or the op-ed page across the way. One paper, the *Niagara Falls* (Ontario) *Review,* has gone even further to accommodate reader contributions. The publication has established a dictating service, available by telephone all day long, whereby a reader with something to say can simply call in, dictate his comments, and hang up; a secretary later transcribes the message, and it is considered for publication (presumably after an authenticity check has been completed).

All of this attention to the letters section is justified, not only because of the importance of preserving the last remaining people's forum, but also because it constitutes one of the publication's most valuable and best-attended features, as the editors well realize.

NOTES

1. Daniel Green, "'Dear Mr. Editor, You Fink': Masses of Letters Deluge Nation's Newspapers as Readers Speak Out," *National Observer,* May 4, 1970.

2. Quoted in Irving Rosenthal, "Who Writes the 'Letters to the Editor'?" *Saturday Review,* September 13, 1969, pp. 114–116.

3. Robert H. Yoakum, "What the *Times* Could Learn from London Letters Pages," *Columbia Journalism Review,* Fall 1970, pp. 50–52.

4. Quoted in A. Kent MacDougall, "Letters to Editor Rise and Beleaguered Press Gives Them More Room," *Wall Street Journal,* August 31, 1970, pp. 1 and 17.

5. G. L. Vacin, "A Study of Letter Writers," *Journalism Quarterly,* Summer 1965, pp. 464–465.

6. David L. Grey and Trevor R. Brown, "Letters to the Editor: Hazy Reflections of Public Opinion," *Journalism Quarterly,* Autumn 1970, pp. 450–456; 471.

7. Rosenthal, *op. cit.,* pp. 114–115.

8. From a symposium, "Letters to the Editor: Perils, Pitfalls and Profits of a Major Feature," *Bulletin of the American Society of Newspaper Editors,* November 1, 1958, pp. 1–3.

9. MacDougall, *op. cit.,* p. 17.

10. Rosenthal, *op. cit.,* p. 116.

11. MacDougall, *op. cit.,* p. 1.

12. *Bulletin, op. cit.,* p. 2.

13. "How Skeptical Are Readers and Why?" *News Research Bulletin* No. 21, American Newspaper Publishers Association, November 19, 1970, p. 74.

13
Editorials in Pictorial Form

A single editorial cartoonist, one theory runs, decided the outcome of the 1960 presidential race between Nixon and Kennedy. Throughout his two terms as vice president, Richard Nixon had been a favorite and frequent target of the brilliant, biting cartoonist of the *Washington Post,* Herbert Block, whose cartoons appear over the signature "Herblock" and are widely syndicated. In Herblock's cartoons Nixon was almost invariably a bad guy, his five o'clock shadow heavily accentuated, his prominent nose emphasized—in short, a blue-jowled thug, up to no good.

One cartoon in particular had infuriated Nixon as the campaign was about to get under way. It depicted a political street rally in the background, with persons holding signs and gathered around a speaker's stand. In the foreground of the cartoon was Nixon climbing up out of a sewer manhole, and one person in the crowd was calling excitedly to the others: "Here he comes now."

This had reference to a repeated Herblock theme: that Nixon had been a dirty fighter in his California campaigning before he became vice president and that he never had shaken off his old ways completely.

In any case, this and other efforts from the pen of the *Post* cartoonist made an understandably deep impression on the vice president, by then the Republican presidential candidate. Some of the worst of the cartoons he tried to keep his wife and daughters from seeing.

So when he gathered with his advisers to plot out the strategy of the early phases of the campaign, Nixon was determined somehow to erase the "Herblock image." To that end, a low-key opening for the campaign was planned and carried out. By the time Nixon and his advisers became aware that Kennedy was making strong headway against this approach, showing up as a vigorous, hard-hitting figure by comparison with Nixon's deliberately bland and low-profile stance, it was too late. The vice president came on strong at the end in his familiar and typical style, but the Democratic candidate had taken the initiative and finally took the election as well, by one of the narrowest margins in American political history. Had Nixon not allowed his opponent the running start out of concern for the Herblock image, some theorists contend, he would have been in the White House eight years earlier than January 1969.[1]

Because the margin was so very narrow in 1960, however, a similar case could be made for any one of countless variables involved in the campaign (e.g., Nixon's knee disability in the early weeks, which kept him immobilized for many precious days, or the role of the makeup man who turned Nixon out for the first of the celebrated TV debates looking pale and uncertain in his first face-to-face confrontation with Senator Kennedy).

But even if it can't be shown to have had the pivotal effect, the Herblock image unquestionably had a significant bearing on the tenor of the campaign and perhaps on its outcome. The episode constitutes another instance in a long series that illustrates the dramatic leverage of the editorial cartoon as an instrument of influence. The series goes back a long way, to the "Join or Die" cartoon of colonial days, which showed the American colonies as the severed segments of a snake, and includes the savage caricatures by Thomas Nast that had so much to do with destroying the powerful Tweed ring that dominated Tammany Hall and New York politics in the latter half of the nineteenth century.

The editorial cartoon is part of the arsenal available to the opinion function of the mass media, and it is one of the most pointed and powerful weapons in the lot.

Presumably, most readers of this book are already familiar enough with editorial pages so that no primer introduction to the editorial cartoon is needed. And it is an equally safe assumption that no reader will have come to this book as a budding artist seeking instruction in the techniques of creating editorial cartoons.[2] So in treating the cartoon, this chapter will tread a middle ground. We'll take a look at the editorial cartoon as one manifestation of the opinion function, examine its peculiar strengths and weaknesses, and consider it from the standpoint of the opinion page editor who makes use of it as one part of the overall editorial section. The reader who wants some how-to-do-it guidance will have to turn elsewhere.

BLADE WITHOUT A HANDLE

Like satire, the editorial cartoon is a biting and savage device. It is also, in some respects, a blade without a handle in that it can injure the wielder as well as the target.

As an editorial device, the cartoon deals necessarily in simplified terms with issues that are often complex. It must make its point swiftly and sharply. There is little leeway for the expression of qualifications or for the introduction of shades of gray—the cartoon deals in the blacks and whites of issues.

As the opinion writer well knows, not very many issues distill down easily to such elemental terms. Thus, there is always the chance that the cartoonist's treatment of a subject will be oversimplified, unbalanced, even unfair. The presence of a cartoon and an editorial on the same page and dealing with the same subject can have the effect of blurring over the range of argumentation in the editorial; the reader will come away remembering the simplistic treatment conveyed by the cartoon rather than the more detailed and balanced examination offered in the editorial.

This is both the strength and the weakness of the editorial cartoon as an expression of the opinion function—it cuts deeply, but not always in the right places.

As a by-product of the tendency to oversimplify an issue, the editorial cartoon is likely to create and to sustain *stereotypes.* We all, of course, utilize stereotypes as shortcuts in our attempts to categorize people and issues in our surroundings. But the cartoonist relies on the stereotype heavily, creating new ones to serve his purpose when old ones wear out from constant use. And in this reliance on the stereotype as a tool of his trade, the cartoonist helps to embed these images deep in the public consciousness (as Herblock did with the sewer-dwelling figure of Nixon, or as Nast did with his depiction of Boss Tweed as a vulture preying on the people of New York).

Some of the stereotypes with which the cartoonists work are stock figures off the shelf, familiar and harmless now: Uncle Sam, the tall, goateed gentleman in the top hat and frock coat; John Q. Public, the put-upon little man being shaken down for his last tax dollar; and Father Time, with robe and hourglass, writing in his Great Book to record the ending of another year, or the passage of a celebrated figure from the stage.

If such stereotypes are relatively harmless (even if outdated), some others are not. The standard depiction of blacks in cartoons as wide-lipped, wide-eyed comic figures out of a minstrel show persisted for many years, as did various other ethnic representations that were deeply offensive to the groups involved. They felt, and very rightly, that the fostering of stereotypical impressions encouraged racism and delayed the acceptance of ethnic groups in American society.

More recently, students and others who had organized to protest American involvement in the Vietnam War found it necessary also to protest the frequent depiction of their numbers in editorial cartoons as consisting entirely of frowzily bearded, wild-eyed, drug-popping crazies. (It must be conceded though that editorial writers, by *their* generalizations and oversimplifications, also contributed to the creation of that particular stereotype.)

Many contemporary editorial cartoonists have to a large extent abandoned the stock figures of Uncle Sam and company, although some of them foster other, newer stereotypical devices. But the most effective of the present-day practitioners depend less on props of any kind than they do on the art of caricature.

Draper Hill, editorial cartoonist for the Memphis *Commercial Appeal,* put the case well for this school:

> This fundamental ingredient, caricature, is too often unappreciated, misunderstood, or confused with burlesque, slapstick and other blunt instruments in the cartoonist's arsenal. Caricature (from L. *caricare:* to lead or charge) is not so much a type of drawing as it is a language of exaggeration.
>
> It rests on a free exercise of the same principles of understanding, selection and emphasis which have animated the greatest achievements in "serious" portraiture. The province of the editorial cartoonist extends beyond the application of this process to faces and figures; it is inextricably concerned with the caricature of situations and attitudes.[3]

It is caricature that lends immediate bite to the work of such contemporary masters as Bill Mauldin of the *Chicago Sun-Times,* Herblock of the *Washington Post,* Paul Conrad of the *Los Angeles Times,* and Pat Oliphant of the *Denver Post.* They are greatly skilled at the art of exaggerated portraiture, but as Hill points out, the caricaturist goes beyond faces and figures. He depicts situations as well.

NOT JUST FUNNY FACES

Herblock shows two senators walking down a corridor past an open door. Inside is a pile of reeking garbage, cans overturned, a black ooze seeping out the door. The title on the door is "Internal Security Sub-committee," and one senator, holding a handkerchief to his nose, is asking the other, "Do you think we should notice it?" In this instance, there is no caricature in the sense usually understood by the layman—exaggeration of a familiar person's features. But there is fine caricature in the broader sense suggested by Draper Hill—and also a highly effective editorial cartoon.

The gifted caricaturist has little need for the labels, balloons, dialogue, and off-the-shelf props that characterize the work of more pedestrian cartoonists. He can convey his editorial themes by means of his art. But the criticism of oversimplification of complex issues can apply to the work of the great cartoonists as well as to that of the lesser ones.

ARE THEY GETTING THROUGH?

Measuring the impact of the editorial cartoon as an instrument of influence is as complex a matter as similar efforts to gauge the effect of editorials. We can single out dramatic individual instances such as Herblock's sewer image, just as we can point to Greeley's "On to Richmond!" editorials as a probable cause of a Civil War battle. But developing the basis for general conclusions about the effectiveness of cartoons as producers of attitude change is not easy.

One study by Del Brinkman of the University of Indiana focused on the question of whether editorials and cartoons on the same subject reinforce each other as agents of attitude change. He presented various combinations of editorials and editorial cartoons to a series of test groups and came to a number of conclusions. Among them was one that cartoons presented with editorials (when both reflect the same theme) will bring about greater opinion change than the presentation of the editorial alone or the cartoon alone. This conforms to common-sense expectations.

But another of his findings was that an editorial presented alone to a test group produced greater opinion change and closure (firming of beliefs or attitudes) than did the presentation of a cartoon alone. In other words, the cartoon may have more dramatic and immediate impact than the editorial, but may not bring about as much attitude change as the more elaborate, balanced approach of the case making in words.[4]

As with other research findings discussed earlier in this book, this one should be considered in perspective. It stemmed from a controlled experiment in laboratory circumstances, and whether it applies generally to the situation represented by the mass communication process is open to argument.

Another study sought to determine whether the cartoonist's ideas were getting over to his audience as he intended them to. LeRoy M. Carl of Temple University took an array of cartoons by 18 of the country's leading editorial cartoonists and asked a random sample of persons in three towns in New York and Pennsylvania what the cartoonist was trying to say in each instance.

The interviews were conducted over a short period of time so that the cartoon subjects would be fresh and timely. The researchers obtained from the cartoonists their own interpretations of the intended messages of the cartoons. Then they found out how accurately these messages had been received by the readers being interviewed.

In two of the communities, the researchers found that only about 15 percent of the respondents saw the cartoonist's intended message clearly, 15 percent got at least part of the message, and an astounding 70 percent misinterpreted altogether the point the cartoonist was trying to make.

> For example, a cartoon showing "Jim Crow" black birds flying north meant "northern migration of Negroes" to many more persons than it meant "increased northern bigotry," the intention of the artist. A cartoon showing Lester Maddox holding an ax handle in one hand and an elephant trunk in another drew a variety of meanings in the small-town study, none of which were in agreement with the cartoonist's meaning. And a cartoon showing President Johnson being warmly received in Manila was judged as a cold reception or snub of the President by most persons.[5]

In the third community, Ithaca, New York, which is the home of Cornell University, the researchers found a slightly better comprehension rate. In Ithaca, 22 percent of those interviewed perceived the cartoon messages as the artists had intended them, 15 percent got the message in part, but 63 percent either didn't understand at all or totally misrepresented the intent of the cartoonist.

As the researcher concluded, "Newspaper editorial cartoonists are communicating with only a small percentage of the readers—at least in three U.S. communities."

Again, of course, the matter must be looked at in perspective. The study did apply to only three communities, not to all readers; it dealt with the work of 18 cartoonists, not all cartoonists, and not just the best cartoonists. Nevertheless, the figures are overwhelming enough to shake the confidence even of a Herblock. Presumably there will be follow-up studies that will explore the impact of editorial cartoons more fully and perhaps offer more encouragement to the artists than did this one. And, of course, it could be argued that if the cartoonist is reaching even 15 or 20 percent of his audience with his message undistorted he is probably doing as well as, or better than, his counterparts at the editorial typewriter.

SOME LIKE IT COLD...

Whatever the research figures say now, or may say later, it seems likely that the editorial cartoon will continue to be a part of the opinion function of the mass media. The generalized indexes we have of reader interest—letters of reaction, readership ratings, and the like—persuade editors that the editorial cartoon is a well-attended feature of the editorial page. As one such editor put it:

> 1. One well drawn, easily understood, imaginatively conceived cartoon is equal in influence to 60 column inches by the opinion-writing staff—even on the opinion writers' rare day of inspired work.
> 2. Most newspaper cartoons aren't well drawn, easily understood or imaginatively conceived.[6]

The editor, Forrest M. Landon of the *Roanoke* (Va.) *Times and World-News,* went on to point out that when they are good, like the little girl with the curl, the cartoonists are very, very good. But not many are that good.

His observation points up an interesting fact about editorial cartooning—it is an art practiced by a tiny circle of professionals; most estimates are that fewer than 200 persons are engaged full time in the production of editorial cartoons in the entire United States.[7]

This means that few newspapers can boast of their very own editorial cartoonist; it also explains why so many of the best cartoonists are widely syndicated. Presumably there are many more than 200 artists who are involved in editorial cartooning on an occasional, part-time, or free-lance basis. But the central core of the art is a very compact group.

In that small company there are the truly great artists, some of whom have already been mentioned in this chapter. And there are also a more numerous group of journeymen whose run-of-the-mill output would have to be characterized as bland rather than biting. Some of these are syndicated, too. They represent men-for-all-philosophies in that they typically tackle very general topics and treat those topics in a deliberately vague and inoffensive fashion. Thus their work can find a comfortable home on a conservative editorial page as well as on a liberal one, perhaps with a slight change of caption.

Those editorial page editors (the vast majority) who do not have a resident cartoonist will typically buy from the syndicates the output of several artists and then select each day the best or most appropriate panel for the day. Depending on the quality of the artist and the circulation size of the purchasing paper, from three to five cartoons a week can be had from a syndicate for from $10 to $100.

As Landon of the Roanoke paper put it, "Lacking a house cartoonist, we buy three from the syndicates: Sanders, Fischetti, Stayskal. On days when Fischetti and Sanders are bad (outdated, cliché ideas, unfathomable, vicious, or out in left field) we throw 'em out; Stayskal, non-ideological and understated, almost always then fills the void."[8]

The *Columbia* (S.C.) *State* uses three syndicated artists: Don Hesse of the *St. Louis Globe-Democrat,* L. D. Warren of the *Cincinnati Enquirer,* and Hugh Haynie of the *Louisville Courier-Journal.* The *St. Louis Post-Dispatch* uses its own Thomas Englehardt, but also works in Herblock and a *Post-Dispatch* alumnus, Bill Mauldin. The *Kalamazoo* (Mich.) *Gazette* uses Herblock, Paul Conrad, and the National Editorial Association and *Chicago Tribune* cartoonists.

Thus the cartoon diet available to a given editorial page editor on a given day may be considerably varied. He can choose from among the pungent and pointed (Herblock, Oliphant, Haynie, Mauldin, Conrad) or from among the men-for-all-philosophies, whose work will not rock the boat that day.

Syndicated editorial cartoonists crop up in magazines, too; and some magazines have staff cartoonists whose work adds a dimension to the opinion function as they use it. There has been some experimentation with cartoons on television (stations in San Francisco, Portland, Oreg., and Charlotte, N.C., have appointed cartoonists as permanent staff members). Set within the swift-moving context of television, however, the cartoon conveys a static impression; on a page of print, the cartoon enjoys the advantage.

In some publications, photographs have been used either regularly or occasionally as substitutes for the editorial cartoon. (We noted earlier, of course, the use of whole pages of photographs as an editorial variant.) But it takes a rather remarkable single photograph to take the place of a cartoon, with its peculiar impact.

In the eyes of at least one cartoonist, Scott Long of the *Minneapolis Tribune*, the photograph poses no serious threat:

> Photographs can never take the place of political cartoons on the editorial pages of the nation's press, although, indeed, they can be used as harmless substitutes.
>
> For a cartoon and a photograph are two entirely different things and the only attribute they have in common is that they are both pictures. . . . A political cartoon is a signed, graphic editorial . . . a cartoon tries to make a point quickly and with wit. It is a subjective judgment of people and events and, if the reader cannot find an opinion in it, the cartoonist obviously has failed.
>
> A photograph, however, is an objective illustration. It is a scientific, graphic presentation of physical facts which offers no interpretation of those facts, but leaves it to the reader to draw his own conclusions from them. Publishers, editors, the public and even some cartoonists tend to confuse a cartoon with an illustration. Nothing could be further from the truth.[9]

On one point, at least, Mr. Long would find little argument—the editorial cartoon, when it is well done, is by no means simply an illustration. It is a significant and integral part of the opinion function and, at its best, an art form of the highest order.

NOTES

1. The discussion of the Herblock image is adapted from T. H. White's *The Making of the President,* 1960, New York, Atheneum, 1961.

2. If that is what he wants, there are some good sources to which he can turn, including Roy Paul Nelson's excellent *Fell's Guide to the Art of Cartooning,* New York, Frederick Fell, 1962.

3. Draper Hill, "Atmosphere of Freedom Is Helpful," *Masthead,* Summer 1971, pp. 6–8.

4. See Del Brinkman, "Do Editorial Cartoons and Editorials Change Opinions?" *Journalism Quarterly,* Winter 1968, pp. 724–726.

5. LeRoy M. Carl, "Editorial Cartoons Fail to Reach Many Readers," *Journalism Quarterly,* Autumn 1968, pp. 533–535.

6. Forrest M. Landon, "Effective Cartoons Clearly A Plus," *Masthead,* Summer 1971, pp. 2–3.

7. According to Hy Rosen, editorial cartoonist for the *Albany* (N.Y.) *Times-Union,* there are only 135 full-time editorial cartoonists in the United States and another 15 in Canada. He made the estimate in a speech to the American Press Institute at Columbia University on May 16, 1972.

8. Landon, *op. cit.,* p. 2.

9. Scott Long, "The Cartoon Is a Weapon," *Masthead,* Fall 1961, pp. 16–18.

14
The 801st Lifetime

In his book, *Future Shock,* Alvin Toffler points out that change in our lives is now taking place at so rapid a rate that most of us cannot assimilate it, cannot even comprehend its pace or scope.

To dramatize his thesis, Toffler divides the most recent 50,000 years of man's existence on earth into 800 lifetimes of approximately 62 years each. Of these 800 lifetimes up to now, 650 were spent in caves. The transmission of information and ideas from one lifetime to another, by means of writing, has been possible only in the last 70 lifetimes. The printed word became available to most of mankind only in the last six. Precise measurement of time became possible only in the last four. The electric motor arrived in the last two. And nearly all of the goods and appliances that we use today were developed in this present, our own, lifetime.

But the headlong acceleration of the pace of change is continuing and is threatening to put us all into a state of shock. Toffler predicts:

> In the three short decades between now and the twenty-first century, millions of ordinary, psychologically normal people will face an abrupt collision with the future. Citizens of the world's richest and most technologically advanced nations, many of them will find it increasingly painful to keep up with the incessant demand for change that characterizes our time. For them, the future will have arrived too soon. . . . Future shock is the dizzying disorientation brought on by the premature arrival of the future. It may well be the most important disease of tomorrow.[1]

If Mr. Toffler's provocative and unsettling prediction is borne out (and he makes a compelling case that it will be), what will be the role of the opinion writer in this period of blinding change? To most of the readers of this textbook, the 801st lifetime is the one that matters. What is the prospect for the opinion function and those who would like to try a hand at wielding it during the next several decades?

(The author may as well make an acknowledgment and a disclaimer at this point. He feels more than a little uneasy about venturing into the realm of prophecy in a medium as slow-paced as a textbook. The time lags of book publishing and of textbook use are such that these words will be coming before the reader a year, two years, or five years after they are written. No prophet likes to have that kind of built-in check on the accuracy of his vision. Predictions are much safer if they can be written in sand or disseminated in some similarly short-lived medium so that by the time the predicted events are supposed to be happening, no one will very clearly remember which guesses were right and which wrong. There are hazards in everything, however, even crossing the street. So let's have at it. But the reader may now consider himself on notice that this chapter is built not on scientific findings or statistics but on informed speculation. *Caveat emptor.*)

MORE NEED THAN EVER

One prediction, at least, can be advanced with some confidence—the opinion function will have greater importance and greater emphasis than ever before as we move on into the era of accelerating change and future shock.

If even now the public is drowning in data and bewildered by the glut of events, the problem promises to become far worse in the years ahead. Not only will the *amount* of information increase exponentially, but the means of disseminating it will also be improved upon, so that greater and greater volume will be on tap. The need for someone to help sort it all out—explain, analyze, point up significance, identify values—will be more urgent than ever.

In his book, *The Information Machines, Their Impact on Men and the Media,* Ben H. Bagdikian pictures a time soon to come when central information consoles will be in living rooms, making available vastly increased ranges of news and information. The consumer will be able to call up, at the press of a button, not only personalized information about products or services he might be interested in buying, but also detailed and exhaustive treatments of news developments of special interest to him but not of such widespread interest that they would warrant inclusion in a mass circulation newspaper. This access to greater depth of information will be made possible by cable TV and its numerous channels, coupled with printout equipment that will allow the consumer to make permanent copies of televised information he finds of particular value. And in all this, Bagdikian sees an expanded role for the opinion function:

> Background and analysis of news will dominate, a tendency already begun. The printed document offers the most attractive setting for such information, compared with voice alone or film or moving words on a screen. It is this kind of journalism that is least perishable in hour-by-hour competition with the broadcast media.[2]

The multiple channels of the home information console will enable the consumer to listen in on city council meetings, congressional committee hearings, or court trials. This will serve to make him aware of additional facets of the world around him and increase still more his need for explanation, background, analysis—in short, the opinion function.

As we have earlier noted, increasing the availability of information does not automatically result in greater understanding. Such understanding may come only with the addition of other dimensions, analysis among them.

McGeorge Bundy, of Harvard and the State Department, made that point effectively in a talk delivered in Washington to the 1967 meeting of the American Society of Newspaper Editors. He was cataloging what to him seemed to be the several levels of news. There is, he said, the public news that consists of overt, surface developments; the backstage news that gets out to the public by accident or design; and a third variety:

> The third kind of news, which I think is the hardest and most important, is the news that cannot be made or reported without thought and study and extensive private talk. It is the news that no one understands until a thoughtful man writes it: the news of analysis. It is where the open road to power is today. And the most remarkable single fact about the men of talent in the rising press is that so many of them, even in 1967, would rather break a story than understand it. Yet it is the others—few as they are— who have the key to power in that their understanding of reality itself becomes the news we want to read.[3]

In Toffler's swift-moving new world, there will be infinitely more stories that will be incomprehensible until "a thoughtful man" analyzes them.

DOUBLE-TRUCKING

But the Toffler world may be a little while coming (he sees the greatest change likely to be accomplished within three decades), and the home information console that Bagdikian talks about is not around the corner just yet. So what about the interim? What forecasts can be made for the short run?

One is that the opinion sections of the various mass media as we now know them will undergo considerable expansion, in large part to allow for the inclusion of greater diversity, more voices.

This is a fairly safe prediction to venture, even in a textbook, since the pattern has already taken recognizable shape in one respect: the marked recent increase in use of the op-ed page for various forms of opinion copy.

The op-ed page is not really new as a journalistic institution. It was a feature of the old *New York World* in the 1920s, when the editors found themselves with more columns and interpretive articles than could be accommodated on the traditional single editorial page. So they expanded to double-truck size (two facing pages), with the traditional editorials still on the left-hand page and with columnists, run-over letters to the editor, and background articles opposite. But the *World* came to an end in 1931 (swallowed up in a merger) without its expanded format having caught on with editorial page editors generally, and it was not until the 1960s that the op-ed idea began to spread.

The *Cleveland Plain-Dealer* instituted a daily op-ed page in 1962, and the *Detroit News* followed suit in 1968. Not all the new versions were the same in content and structure, however, as a contemporary authority on editorial writing, Hillier Krieghbaum of New York University, noted in a 1971 article:

> Despite the *World's* generation-old tradition, the term "op-ed" currently has several distinct, and decidedly different, meanings. Conventionally it is used to describe that page opposite the one on which the paper's own editorial views are printed. But the *Chicago Tribune*'s "Perspective" is two pages beyond the editorials, not facing. For the Tucson, Phoenix, and Indianapolis papers of Eugene C. Pulliam, the op-ed page, while facing the

editorials, is used as space for publishing views opposite to those stated in editorials, and it carries the heading "As Others See It." At the Louisville *Courier-Journal,* the page facing editorials is marked "Dimension, a Page of Background, Interpretation and Commentary," and that is exactly what it is for local, regional, national, and world issues. On a few papers, the op-ed materials are simply columns added to those of the editorial page itself, and if presses and readers would accept ten- or twelve-column-wide pages, that would be the way the whole presentation would be made. For these dailies, op-ed is simply an annex without special requirements. The majority, however, have distinctive approaches.[4]

The most significant of the new op-ed pages is perhaps that of the *New York Times,* a publication that has been typically slow to take up innovations. But in 1970 the *Times* joined the trend, and before a year had passed *Time* magazine described the new feature as not only "one of the most closely-watched and sought-after forums for comment in U.S. daily journalism but probably the best Op-Ed page anywhere."[5]

The reasoning behind the *Times*'s decision to expand its opinion section is the same as that advanced by some of the other papers that have taken the step in recent years—to widen the range of opinions available to its readers. The editor of the page, Harrison E. Salisbury, says:

> The horizon of Op-Ed is just about as broad as the world's. The theory is that anything which a *Times* reader should know about, anything which may have been neglected or not yet brought to light concerning the human condition, is a fit subject for the page—provided it is brightly and sharply written. If the author has a critical viewpoint, a case that must be argued hard, a case which should be heard (even if not agreed with), he is in our ballpark.[6]

The size of the ballpark is emphasized by the nature of some of the contributions that have appeared. They have included essays by Chancellor Willy Brandt of West Germany, Black Panther Richard Moore writing from exile in Algiers, Charles Reich (*The Greening of America*), and Herbert Marcuse, philosopher to the New Left and the alienated young. There have also been many contributions from less celebrated figures. As *Time* noted:

> The most inflammatory essay to date was an open letter to his college-bound son by a Southern physician, Dr. Paul Williamson.

Stick to studying and necking and avoid revolution, wrote the father, or "expect to get shot. Mother and I will grieve, but we will gladly buy a dinner for the National Guardsman who shot you." More than 300 letters poured in to the *Times,* most of them attacking the doctor.[7]

Many of the contributions to the op-ed page at the *Times* are solicited by the editor, but many others come in over the transom. And the impact of the essays, columns, or letters on the page is not limited to initial publication. Salisbury estimated in early 1971, after the experiment had been under way less than nine months, that "at least 100 books have been commissioned or proposed thus far to authors who appear on Op-Ed."[8]

But not all the new voices that will be heard in expanded opinion sections will be those from outside the publication. Various straws swirling by in the wind suggest that the long established practice of having policy formulated and articulated by a small circle of full-time specialists may be modified in various ways in the near future.

OTHER VOICES, OTHER ROOMS

One such straw is a proposal advanced in the *Chicago Journalism Review,* a journal of press criticism edited by staff members of Chicago newspapers and wire services. A *Review* editor proposed that analysis and opinion pieces for the editorial section ought to come occasionally from the newsroom as well as the editorial room. He cited several instances in which the published comment of Chicago and Washington editorial writers was sharply at variance with the facts as they had been reported by the respective newspapers' reporters or Washington correspondents. And the *Review* writer, Dan Rottenberg, continued:

> The traditional objection to letting reporters write editorials is that it will hurt their relationships with news sources by undermining their objectivity; also, that a reporter who publicly takes a position on an issue will become an apologist for that position in his subsequent reporting of the issue. Both objections are valid if we stick to the old definition of the purpose of an editorial: to promote a point of view. If, on the other hand, the editorial column is viewed as a place where professional newsmen seek to shed light on a problem, there should be no danger. . . .
> Regardless of the stand a newspaper takes, the reader is better served if the editorial writer knows what he is talking about. In

many cases the way to achieve a well-informed editorial is to let a reporter write it—assuming, of course, that the reporter is a professional who will place the reader's interest above his own personal feelings.[9]

And a few additional straws:

Straw 2.   The *Rochester Democrat and Chronicle* in 1970 began the practice of adding to its regular editorial conference two reporters from the newsroom. The reporter participation was on a rotating basis, usually for two-week periods. The reporters took full part in the discussions of editorial policy questions.[10]

Straw 3.   The *London* (Ontario) *Free Press* for a period during 1971 and 1972 assigned men and women from the newsroom to two- and three-week stints on the editorial page staff. The assignees included persons from all areas of the news staff, from women's editors to beat reporters. They wrote editorials as well as contributed to the policy discussion, and they also were welcome contributors to a local, signed opinion column carried on the editorial page.[11]

Straw 4.   The *Dayton Daily News,* an evening daily with a circulation of 60,000, in 1970 had a three-man editorial page staff. The editor of the page was 35. The other two writers were 30 and 28. This constituted a striking departure from the traditional pattern on editorial pages. The writers typically have been men who had come up through the chairs and the years and had achieved a senior-statesman kind of status within the newspaper organization. A profile of the members of the National Conference of Editorial Writers developed by Dr. Edwin Emery of the University of Minnesota and published in 1963 portrayed the typical editorial writer as a man of about 50 who had been in the newspaper business about 27 years and in editorial page work for about 12 years.[12]   A similar survey conducted in 1971 showed that the median age of the editorial writers had moved down to 48.4.[13]   The three at Dayton could not have accounted for that much shift in the overall population, so it would appear that some new and younger blood is coming into the editorial rooms. And the trend, it seems likely, will continue. (However, it must be noted that the average age of the editorial board of the *New York Times* in 1970 was 51, and the youngest member was 41. The youth movement isn't spreading *that* fast.)[14]

Straw 5.   There is also the experiment (noted in Chapter 9) of the *National Observer,* which has replaced the conventional editorial columns with a roundup of "Observations" written and signed by various members of the magazine's staff—not just editorial writers.

The straws are numerous enough, varied enough, and widely enough scattered so that the movement to bring new voices into the editorial rooms is apparent. How those new voices will be blended into the well-rehearsed editorial choruses now in operation will vary from paper to paper, situation to situation. But some new and different notes are going to be heard, that much seems sure.

STRAIGHT STUFF OR BLENDS?

One final, fearless prediction for the future of the opinion function: There will be in the years to come a spreading out of the opinion function into all parts of the publication or the broadcast mix, not only in a physical sense but in terms of increasing catholicity of subject matter.

The rationale for this spreading out will be the growing demand of the consumer for more insight into the meaning of the flow of events in Toffler's accelerating new world. The expansion of the conventional editorial sections just discussed may meet the problem momentarily; the home information console hooked to data banks manned by specialists in analysis will be the answer in the long run. In between, there will be a time when there won't be enough space in the conventional editorial sections—even after expansion. And the reader or viewer will become impatient and confused if he has to turn from the news item to some segregated section elsewhere to find out what it means. So, whether we like it or not, the prospect is that opinion will become an ever larger factor in the overall mix of information and ideas provided by the various media of mass communication.

If you accept that assumption, the crucial question becomes: How will the mix be blended? Will it turn out to be something like *Time* magazine's unlabeled, predigested mixture of fact and opinion? Will the concept of journalism of advocacy, that new incarnation of interpretive reporting with an overlay of opinion, be the wave of the future? Or will there still be some way to observe a truth-in-packaging philosophy and put before the consumer honestly labeled, clearly differentiated news and opinion?

The easy way would be to accept the blend approach, concede that Henry Luce and the activists (unlikely bedfellows) were right and let the consumer fend for himself. But it seems to the author that there are several other perfectly feasible possibilities, all of which would allow for the labeling of opinion and yet would meet the need of consumers for more—and for more immediately accessible—analysis of the news.

The fact that these other possibilities haven't as yet been given a trial should not rule them out of consideration. So let's consider them.

SHIRTTAILS

One such possibility has been talked of now and then by editors or professors, but not—at least not to the author's knowledge—been given a trial. This is the shirttail editorial.

The shirttail editorial would not appear on the editorial page but, as its name suggests, would be tucked in at the end of the news item to which it referred. It would be separated from the news story by a line dash and a short label head. The reader would then move directly from consideration of the facts of the news to an analysis of those facts, and he would know which was which. The TV broadcasters provide the equivalent of this now, when they come to the screen immediately after a presidential address to provide what Vice President Spiro Agnew attacked as "instant analysis."

The shirttail editorial has some obvious drawbacks (the reader will note that we're following the two-sided presentation approach here). It calls for some very close coordination between the news department and the editorial writers in the newsroom, as part of the staff. And because the deadline situation with news items is typically tight, the analyst would have little time for research before he had to crank out his instant analysis.

But there would be some economies, too. The opinion writer would not have to waste any time or space sketching in background—all the news facts would be right above him in the column, and fresh in the reader's mind. And with the increasing use of computers for information storage and retrieval, the shirttail writer could shortcut research processes considerably. The advantage to the reader would be obvious— the questions raised in his mind by the complexities of the news would be answered at once, not in some distant section of the paper or on a later broadcast.

CROSS-REFERENCING

Another possibility is somewhat more intricate and comes closer to *Time*'s advocacy approach. It would involve rewriting portions of news stories so as to incorporate in them quotations from expressions of opinion made on the subject in the news at some earlier time. In other words, a writer working in the newsroom, at the elbow of the wire editor, would pick out two or three stories that called for analysis. Then he would use the publication's data retrieval system to call up any editorial comment made by the paper in some previous issue and dealing with the topics of the current news developments. In the same manner, he could bring to hand comments of columnists or commentators that might be relevant. Then he could rewrite portions of the news story, weaving in references to these other analytical comments. For example:

> A *Journal* editorial writer, commenting on an earlier development in the international monetary crisis observed last April:
> "What is pending now is a wholesale retreat from gold or any other fixed monetary standard. . . ."

This would help to give the latest development meaning to the reader, provided that the analyst–rewrite man was doing a sound and skillful job of selecting previously published opinion to work into the story. Without the jog to his memory, the reader couldn't be expected to recall some of those earlier comments that would be enlightening in view of the most recent news break.

This approach to expanding the opinion function would still preserve the labeling philosophy, although admittedly the reader would have to be paying close attention. As with the shirttail, the cross-referencing system would involve some careful coordinating between news and editorial departments, the availability of computers, and the presence of opinion writers who were deeply informed in their subject areas.

TWO FOR THE PRICE OF ONE

Yet another approach has been suggested, not by an editor or educator, but by a medical man, Dr. John E. Tysell. Now an Oregon physician, Tysell grew up in a small-town newspaper family in South Dakota and acquired a feel for the newspaper traditions his publisher-father honored. In a letter to an Oregon editor, Dr. Tysell advanced the proposal that in this day of monopoly or semimonopoly journalism, and at a time when we need opinion as well as fact to help us on our way to judgment and conclusion, any newspaper ought to have *two* editorial pages and two editorial staffs, not one.

Tysell proposed that the editor deliberately seek out and hire two sets of editorial writers having sharply different ideological bents. And then, when a controversial subject comes up, let both groups have at it and spread their contending arguments before the reader. This would certainly be in keeping with the philosophy of Milton and of John Stuart Mill—that, in the clash of views in an open marketplace of ideas, the truth would be discernible. It would also considerably increase the newspaper's editorial budget, of course, but if we accept the fact that the consumer is going to be demanding more and more analysis, some such budgetary allocation will have to be made in any case.

The editors who go out of their way to select columnists whose views differ from those of the publication are in one sense making a gesture toward the two-barreled approach that Dr. Tysell proposed. But, as was noted earlier, not very many editors choose columnists as counterbalance; more often, they are chosen to reinforce the paper's position.

These several proposals for ways in which the opinion function could be expanded and spread out into the overall content of the mass media of communication are admittedly unorthodox and far-out in terms of what is now being done. But what is now being done simply may not much longer serve the consumer's needs; in fact, it may not be serving them right now, even before Mr. Toffler's disconcerting predictions have been realized. So, offbeat or not, the several proposals above at least deserve to be considered as among the options available. They might be preferable to the alternative of increased doses of *Time*-style interpretation or the unlabeled advocacy of the activists.

A FINAL WORD

During the nearly three decades since The Bomb came on the scene, all of us have lived against a backdrop of potential apocalypse. Generations have come of age aware that the world as we know it could, in the space of a few hours, be reduced to radioactive cinder. Simultaneously, we have been experiencing the acceleration of change of which Toffler writes, leaving us in one stage or another of future shock. In many who have lived through this period, and are living in it now, these overwhelming facts of life have bred a sense of helplessness and hopelessness. It would be ludicrous in the circumstances to suggest that the opinion function of the mass media of communication provides any universal, one-size-fits-all answer to the bewilderment and confusion with which we all must contend; the editorialist is no white knight riding to the rescue of mankind as the sound track builds to a crescendo in the background.

But it is *not* ludicrous, it is *not* unreasonable, to argue that the gyroscope effect of the opinion function constitutes one of our best remaining hopes of achieving a sense of balance and perspective in the face of towering apprehensions and a suffocating glut of information and ideas.

Erwin Canham, the editor of the *Christian Science Monitor,* was addressing himself particularly to newspaper editors in the following comment. But it applies as well to the opinion writers of all of the mass media. His plea was for better thinking, for a more vigorous and imaginative exercise of the opinion function:

> What do I mean by better thinking? Simply that human society in our time, and the printed word with it, is in danger of being drowned in a tide of sentiment and softness. We live in the greatest age humanity has ever known, and we are not worthy of it. All the human race has ever hoped for is in danger of being blown up, not necessarily by design but ingloriously by accident. That would be an inexcusable end for man. Men who use the sharp and hard tool of the printed word should be using it to awaken humanity to its danger. We need to snap out of our drift. This is a time for great and eloquent voices, not for the coward's whimper or the cynic's whine. Where are the great voices? Sometimes we catch an echo. They should be crying out daily from our newspapers.[15]

They should be crying out daily from *all* of the media of communication. But they must indeed be great voices, informed, honest, and courageous. There is work to be done by the opinion writers—important work, creative work, and deeply gratifying work. They may not be the world's saviors. But they can provide a significant—perhaps an indispensable—assist to those who may fill that role.

NOTES

1. Alvin Toffler, *Future Shock,* New York, Bantam, 1971, pp. 9 and 11.

2. Ben H. Bagdikian, *The Information Machines, Their Impact on Men and the Media,* New York, Harper & Row, 1971.

3. In *Problems of Journalism,* the proceedings of the 1967 convention of the American Society of Newspaper Editors, New York, American Society of Newspaper Editors, 1967, p. 80.

4. Hillier Krieghbaum, "The 'Op-Ed' Page Revisited," *Saturday Review,* November 13, 1971, p. 91.

5. *Time,* June 21, 1971, p. 36.

6. Harrison E. Salisbury, "An Extra Dimension in This Complicated World," *Masthead*, Spring 1971, pp. 29–31.

7. *Time, op. cit.*

8. Salisbury, *op. cit.*, p. 31.

9. Dan Rottenberg, "Who Is Best Qualified to Write Editorials?" *Chicago Journalism Review*, May 1971, pp. 5–6.

10. Desmond Stone, "How Does the News Staff Dissent?" *Masthead*, Spring 1971, p. 24.

11. Terrence W. Honey, "Our Ivory Tower Syndrome Is Dead," *Masthead*, Summer 1971, pp. 20–22.

12. The survey findings are described in detail in "The Editor Goes Status Seeking and Image Hunting," by Wilbur Elston, *Masthead*, Spring 1963, pp. 1–18.

13. Cleveland Wilhoit and Dan Drew, "A Profile of the Editorial Writer," *Masthead*, Fall 1971, pp. 2–14.

14. *Editor and Publisher*, August 22, 1970, p. 22.

15. Erwin D. Canham, "The World Flow of News," *Nieman Reports*, March 1971, p. 10.

A Selected, Annotated Bibliography

The sources cited and briefly described in the listing below are those that the author believes would be particularly useful to any reader of this text who is interested in investigating further the field of opinion writing and the effects of such writing on the mass media audiences.

It is not meant to be definitive, of course. The chapter footnotes in the text constitute, in themselves, a kind of running bibliography considerably more comprehensive than the annotated list that follows.

Bagdikian, Ben H., "How Newspapers Use Columnists," *Columbia Journalism Review,* Fall 1964, pp. 20–24, and "How Editors Pick Columnists," *Columbia Journalism Review,* Spring, 1966, pp. 40–45.

These two articles document the role of columnists in the editorial page mix, evaluate the company of Washington columnists on an ideological spectrum, and report the ways in which editors utilize the syndicated opinion writers to balance or to reinforce the policy of their publications.

_____ , *The Information Machines, Their Impact on Men and the Media,* New York, Harper & Row, 1971.

An absorbing look into the communication technology of the future. There are several passages relating to the role of the opinion function in years to come.

Berelson, Bernard, and Janowitz, Morris, *Reader in Public Opinion and Communication,* 2nd edition, New York, Free Press, 1966.

Several sections of this reader contain material of special relevance to the opinion writer. Among them: a chapter by Lazarsfeld, Berelson, and Gaudet in section 2 on the point at which a voter makes a final decision in a contested election campaign; a chapter, in section 8, by the Langs on the mass media and voting; another by Klapper on the effects of mass communication; and yet another by Katz on attitude change. There is also a helpful though not comprehensive section (11) on research method.

Blume, Norman, and Lyons, Schley, "The Monopoly Newspaper in a Local Election: The Toledo *Blade," Journalism Quarterly,* Summer 1968, pp. 286-292.

In this study two researchers record an attempt to measure in precise terms the impact of newspaper editorial support of a candidate. This is one of the very few such approaches undertaken in quantitative terms, and on the basis of sound methodology.

Boorstin, Daniel J., *The Image,* New York, Harper & Row, 1961.

Though not dealing at any point directly with opinion writing, this absorbing, clearly written analysis of the way in which Americans have become preoccupied with "psuedo-events" created by the press has a good deal to contribute to an editorial writer's understanding of his potential audience. Of particular value: chapters 1, 2, and 4.

Brucker, Herbert, "How to Write an Editorial," *Saturday Review,* February 12, 1966, pp. 58-60.

A former newspaper editor (*Hartford Courant*) offers some thoughtful comments on editorial writing style, the role of the opinion function, and the satisfactions and frustrations that come to the editorial writer.

Bush, Chilton R., *Editorial Thinking and Writing,* New York, Appelton, 1932.

Long out of print, this early textbook on editorial writing nevertheless remains as relevant as ever in its sections dealing with the way we think and with the uses of logic in the development of persuasive arguments (Chapters 4-9 in particular).

—— , ed., *News Research for Better Newspapers,* New York, American Newspaper Publishers Association Foundation. (Published annually prior to vol. 5, biennially thereafter.)

This compilation, in brief, of research findings includes in nearly every volume some studies of interest to opinion writers. Each volume is organized by subject area, which makes scanning for relevant titles an easy matter. The study results are described in layman's language, with a minimum of statistics and jargon.

Carl, Leroy M., "Editorial Cartoons Fail to Reach Many Readers," *Journalism Quarterly,* Autumn 1968, pp. 533-535.

Report of a study showing the disconcerting degree to which readers tend to misinterpret the intended message of the editorial cartoonist.

Elston, Wilbur, "The Editor Goes Status-Seeking and Image-Hunting," *Masthead,* Spring 1963, pp. 1-18.
A profile study of editorial writers and their attitudes toward their work. Some of the statistical material provides a basis for comparison with the findings of the Wilhoit-Drew study made nearly ten years later. (See later entry in this bibliography.)

Frazier, Robert B., "The Editorial Elbow—Being a More-or-Less Compleat Listing of Reference Works Useful, Day by Day, to the Editor, Reporter, and Copyreader," *Masthead,* Summer 1963, pp. 5-16.
An excellent selection, drawn up by an experienced editorial writer who is also a former editor of *Masthead.* The same writer reported on a survey of the magazine- and newspaper-reading habits of editorial writers in another *Masthead* article, "What Do You Read, My Lord?", Summer 1962, pp. 10-16.

Graves, Harold F., and Oldsey, Bernard S., *From Fact to Judgment,* New York, Macmillan, 1957.
Chapters 5-8 of this textbook on writing deal specifically with the problems of analyzing and organizing persuasive arguments and defending judgments once reached. The authors make clear and effective application of basic principles of logic and illustrate their points with examples taken from press and literature.

Karlins, Marvin, and Abelson, Herbert I., *Persuasion,* New York, Springer Publishing Co., 1970.
This is an extremely useful summary of research into the ways in which opinions and attitudes are changed. Major lines of research during the last two decades are noted and specimen studies in each area are briefly sketched and evaluated. The reader is provided with the titles of the original papers, articles, or books in which the specimen studies are reported in full, should he wish to explore.

Krieghbaum, Hillier, *Facts in Perspective,* Englewood Cliffs, N.J., Prentice-Hall, 1956.
This comprehensive text has numerous helpful, illustrative examples of editorials, editorial headlines, columns, and interpretive backgrounders. It deals with editorial page makeup as well as editorial writing.

Laney, Richard B., "How They Run the Shop," *Masthead,* Fall 1965, pp. 23-28.
This summary notes the results of a survey of the ways in which

policy is fashioned and day-by-day decisions are made on the editorial staffs of 220 U.S. dailies.

Lazarsfeld, Paul, Berelson, Bernard, and Gaudet, H., *The People's Choice,* New York, Duell, Sloan & Pearce, 1944.

This is the original report of the studies that led to the development of the two-step flow concept of opinion and information diffusion (later expanded to the *n*-step flow concept).

Lippmann, Walter, *Public Opinion,* New York, Macmillan, 1960.

Lippmann's is the classic, seminal treatment of public opinion for the lay reader, and was first published in 1922. The 1960 paperback edition is the original text, not a revised version. The introductory essay and sections of part III, on stereotypes, are quoted in most of the readers and anthologies in this field. Anyone interested in directing persuasive messages at a mass audience ought to spend some time with the original work.

Lyons, Louis M., *Reporting the News,* Cambridge, Mass., Harvard University Press, 1965.

Several chapters in this anthology of articles from the *Nieman Reports* are of particular interest to opinion writers: "Take a Forthright Stand," by Thomas M. Storke, Pulitzer prize- winning editor; "Editorial Writing Made Easy," by Louis M. Lyons, an examination into a canned-editorial factory; and "Crusading in a Small Town," by Ernest H. Linford. Many other pieces in the book, though not directly pertaining to opinion writing, have much to offer any would-be journalist.

MacDougall, A. Kent, "Letters to the Editor Rise and Beleaguered Press Gives Them More Room," *The Wall Street Journal,* August 31, 1970, pp. 1 and 17.

An interesting, sprightly roundup of comment on the upsurge of reader contributions to the opinion section.

MacDougall, Curtis D., *Understanding Public Opinion,* New York, Macmillan, 1952.

Of interest particularly for the five chapters in part II, "Culture and Public Opinion," which discuss the influence on attitudes exerted by cultural background, legends, myths, taboos, and prejudices.

Meyer, Karl E., *The New America,* New York, Basic Books, 1961.

An editorial writer surveys the current [early 1960s] scene and the role of the mass communications media in shaping that scene. Thoughtful and well written, but not devoted to editorial writing except incidentally.

Nevins, Allan, *American Press Opinion, Washington to Coolidge,* Boston, Heath, 1928.

A selection of editorials, quoted in full, from colonial times to the late 1920s, chosen and introduced by a distinguished historian who also knew the newspaper field well. The book is particularly interesting for its sampling of changing editorial style over nearly two centuries.

Sargent, Dwight, "Twenty Years before the Masthead," *Neiman Reports,* December 1966, pp. 11-14.

A retrospective look at the first two decades of existence of the National Conference of Editorial Writers and its accomplishments. The writer is one of the organization's founders.

Schacht, John H., *The Journals of Opinion and Reportage: An Assessment,* Magazine Publishers Association, 1966.

This monograph provides a descriptive history and analysis of the opinion magazines located on all points of the ideological spectrum.

Schramm, Wilbur, *The Process and Effects of Mass Communication,* Urbana, University of Illinois Press, 1965.

This reader is of interest to editorial writers chiefly for the section on modifying attitudes and opinions, with chapters by Osgood and Tannenbaum on the congruity principle; by Hovland, Lumsdaine, and Sheffield on one-sided vs. two-sided studies; and by Hovland and Weiss on the influence of source credibility on communication effectiveness. A revised 1971 edition of this book, with Donald F. Roberts as coauthor, omits some of the above-mentioned chapters but adds excerpts from Lippmann's treatment of stereotypes, Boorstin's discussion of pseudo-events, and Cartwright's description of the principles of mass persuasion.

Symposium, "The Op-Ed Page Gains in Popularity," *Masthead,* Spring 1971, pp. 29-34.

Opinion page editors of the *New York Times, Milwaukee Journal,* and *Tucson Citizen* describe some experiments they had recently undertaken with op-ed pages. The most interesting contribution is that of Harrison Salisbury of the *Times,* who describes why his paper came to the decision to enlarge the editorial section.

Waldrop, A. Gayle, *Editor and Editorial Writer,* 3rd edition, Dubuque, Iowa, Brown, 1967.

The most recent revision of this long-standard text in the field covers style, editorial construction, variations, makeup, and letters to the editor. The end-of-chapter bibliographies are unusually comprehensive.

Wilhoit, Cleveland, and Drew, Dan, "A Profile of the Editorial Writer," *Masthead,* Fall 1971, pp. 2-14.
The composite editorial writer is statistically depicted by his age, political leanings, educational background, outside entanglements, and attitude toward his work. (*See also* Elston, Wilbur.)

Zimbardo, Philip, and Ebbeson, Ebbe E., *Influencing Attitudes and Changing Behavior,* rev. ed., Reading, Mass., Addison-Wesley, 1970.
This is an effort, largely successful, to present in language understandable to the layman some trends in research into behavioral change. Both the philosophy and the methodology of such research is described, and there is a helpful set of appendixes explaining the ABCs of the scientific method and the techniques of attitude measurement. The book's only defect is its reliance on some rather outdated studies as examples. But the approach is far from outdated; it is lively, provocative, and understandable.

Index

73 74 75   10 9 8 7 6 5 4 3 2 1